AMERICAN VALUES *in the* TRUMP ERA

A Battle for the Soul of America

Jim Boeglin

ARCHWAY
PUBLISHING

Archway Publishing books may be ordered through booksellers or by contacting:

Archway Publishing
1663 Liberty Drive
Bloomington, IN 47403
www.archwaypublishing.com
1 (888) 242-5904

ISBN: 978-1-4808-8349-9 (sc)
ISBN: 978-1-4808-8348-2 (hc)
ISBN: 978-1-4808-8350-5 (e)

Library of Congress Control Number: 2019915925

Print information available on the last page.

Archway Publishing rev. date: 10/11/2019

Dedication

During the Donald J. Trump presidency, America is experiencing an unprecedented time of inner turmoil, deception, obstruction, divisiveness, anger, intimidation, and attack. Traditional American values are changing before our very eyes. Many Americans have become polarized on one side of the tug-of-war or the other. Moderates and centrists are being squeezed out of the discussion. Violence and anger are on the rise. Claims of attempted "political coups" and "treason" are being charged by a president under intense legal and moral scrutiny.

The executive branch and much of Congress are at war with each other. The odor of impeachment hangs in the air. The maligned federal judiciary may hold America's future in its hands. The rule of law and America's democratic form of government are in danger of being replaced by authoritarian rule.

This book is dedicated to the members of the independent free press who, despite daily attacks on their credibility, continue to uphold their daunting responsibility to question and investigate governmental leaders relative to their policies and actions, and to keep American citizens informed.

The legendary Argentine journalist, Andrew Graham-Yooll, who risked his life to report on disappearing critics of the authoritarian regime said it best: "Of course we were afraid. But it's one thing to be afraid, and another thing to be a coward." The free and courageous press is currently the buffer separating American democracy from authoritarianism.

Contents

Introduction

These are not normal times in America, just as the nineteen thirties were not normal times in Germany. Dark forces are at work to change the very essence of what it means to be an American. This is not a time to bury our heads in the sand, believe everything we are told, and deny what is happening. This is a time to be asking critical questions of who we are and what we value, both individually and as a society. What do I stand for? What does America stand for?

President Trump was elected on a campaign slogan to "make America great again." What is the underlying message of this slogan? Just what is it that makes America great? The message implies that America was great at one time but is no longer great. Is Trump trying to take us back to a time when:

➢ White males were in total charge?
➢ A woman's place was in the home?
➢ Races were segregated in housing, education, and opportunity?
➢ Religions dictated social behavior?
➢ Businesses functioned free of regulation?

I suspect that many racial minorities, women, consumers, and environmentalists do not think of those days as the "good old days." Many white males are also not eager to return to the old system.

Military strength, natural resources, factories, and bricks and mortar are nice assets for a nation to have. However, I do not believe that the greatness of America is a matter of its balance sheet of tangible assets and liabilities. I believe the true greatness of America derives from:

> ➤ a stable, democratic form of government;
> ➤ an impartial judicial system designed to provide equal justice for everyone;
> ➤ precious personal freedoms provided by the Constitution and Bill of Rights and protected by the courts;
> ➤ values and traditions based on ethics, morality, and spiritual principles;
> ➤ a history of openness and welcoming that has created diversity among its citizens;
> ➤ a free enterprise system that has allowed business to flourish;
> ➤ unions that have protected rights of workers; and
> ➤ a long history of moral leadership in the world.

These are the intangibles of greatness. Based on these traditional values, America was already great before Trump arrived on the scene. After less than one term as president, America is now in serious danger of losing much of this greatness. These intangibles are the real focus of the tug-of-war playing out in America during the Trump era.

What Drives Us?

Our personal values largely determine how we conduct our daily lives. Values are the ongoing beliefs and ideals of an individual, family, company, religion, group, culture, or society. Values influence attitudes and behaviors, guiding us through our life experience. They determine what we are for and what we are against.

Leadership plays an important role in developing group values—for good or for evil. Too many people are only too happy to be told what to think and what to believe. They are easily influenced and manipulated by powerfully persuasive leaders. Personal values can be short-circuited by misguided leaders and corrupt group values.

Values can be spiritually driven, or they can be ego-driven. It is essentially the difference between love and fear. Most of us move back and forth along the spectrum of love and fear as we go through our human experience of life on planet Earth.

In an individual and a culture that primarily values peace, kindness, honesty, generosity, and truthfulness, it is clear that violence, anger, mean-spirited attacks, blame, lies, obstruction, and deception would not be honored practices. Conversely, if people value aggressive, abusive, bullying behavior from their leaders, an attitude of winning at any cost, with no regard for laws, facts, or the truth, then loving kindness, caring, integrity, fair play, and ethical behavior would be belittled and devalued. We tend to align ourselves with our basic values.

I have a personal theory that a nation's political leadership usually reflects the collective consciousness of its citizens. To a certain extent, we get what we deserve. If the societal majority values fear more than love, it is destined to be governed by fearful, bigoted, dishonest, manipulative leaders who want to wall off the country from the rest of the world—especially those "dangerous" parts of the world that are of different skin color or religious traditions. If the societal majority values cooperation, kindness, diversity, integrity, forming global alliances, extending a loving welcome and openness to others, it is likely to be governed by secure, well-meaning leaders who responsibly understand both the risks and the rewards of sharing and openness.

America in the Trump era is at a crossroads, contemplating which path to take. The nation is strongly conflicted on this future direction. America seems to be in an unsettled and chaotic turmoil, struggling to find a way out of the tug-of-war that is in process. In hindsight, the 2020 elections will be a clue as to which direction we choose to take as a nation.

Values Evolve

Most American values have not been etched in stone. They have evolved and changed over the centuries to reflect societal norms and expectations. Throughout our history, however, there has always been a consistent grounding in such spiritual and religious basics as kindness, respect, honesty, integrity, fair play, and truthfulness. It feels like the centuries-long peaceful evolution has dramatically shifted to a violent, ego-driven revolution in the era of Trump, with traditional values rapidly moving outside of the historic mainstream.

Over time I believe the direction our nation takes will be determined by the predominant values of ordinary Americans, with the leadership of the country ultimately reflecting the collective consciousness of the majority. The ordinary people of America eventually control this decision. Before irreparable harm is done to American values, this may be the time for fair-minded Americans to wise up, speak up, question what they are told, and become engaged in the political process.

Personal Choices

Life is all about choices. In America, every one of us is free to choose our thoughts, which ultimately lead to our values. Values are a consequence of thoughts. Actions are a consequence of values. My own life is an example of choices based on my personal values at the time.

As a teenager I dreamed of being a writer but did not value writing enough to pursue it as a career. I was afraid that I could not make a living and raise a family as a writer. My fears trumped my love for writing. Instead of pursuing journalism as my college major, I opted for economics and then law school. I intentionally delayed my writing career for decades. Eventually, I realized that my lifelong dream of being a writer was slipping away along with my rapidly aging life. It was a matter of "now or never." It was time for me to choose to fully value my dream of writing—or not.

It was a scary decision, but I began sharing my thoughts in writing as a seventy-three-year-old author, fifteen years after my retirement from the practice of law. My first book was published at age seventy-four and a second book followed at seventy-five. The feedback I have received from readers is meaningful and satisfying. It seems I am making a positive difference in some peoples' lives—including my own.

This is book #3 of the Bike Writer Trilogy—so named because so many of the thoughts and ideas that end up in my books bubble to the surface while riding my bike.

Book #1, *The Bike Writer—Insights Discovered along the Bicycle Paths of Life*—uses the bike path as a metaphor for learning from life experiences such as: growing up the youngest of a large family in a small town in the years following World War II; recovering from an early overdose of Catholicism; coping with the death of my dad when I was barely sixteen; working my way through high school, college, and law school; lessons learned while practicing law; surviving an unexpected and painful ending to a twenty-year marriage; taking a second chance on love; serving on boards of not-for-profit organizations; dealing with triple bypass surgery; being acutely aware of the aging process; and yes, bicycling almost every day, including bike trips in at least eleven states of the Union and two weeks on the Romantic Road in Germany.

Book #2, *Character Building—the ABCs of Building Depth and Strength of Character*—addresses the ways in which we as individuals wrestle with developing our "character accounts." How can an ordinary person evolve into a person of character who leads a life of honesty, integrity, truthfulness, respect for others, and has a strong commitment to doing the right thing? Conversely, what kinds of thoughts, values, and choices can cause a person's character account to be overdrawn?

This gets me to book #3. In America, the State of the Union Address has become an annual tradition, delivered by the president to a joint session of Congress. It highlights the accomplishments of the administration, failures of the opposing party, legislative achievements, current conditions of the economy, the status of foreign relations, strength of the military, taxes and the budget, political appointments, issues of the day, momentous judicial decisions, plans for the future, and the like.

This book comes from a different perspective than the State of the Union Address. It isn't based on statistics or numbers. Book #3 subjectively explores the "spiritual consciousness" of the American people and its leaders. In a way, this book is an extension of book #2, expanding the subject of character from the individual to the national level. Does our nation's character account have a healthy balance, or is the account overdrawn? In which direction are we moving?

Questions

I have many more questions than answers:

- ➤ At our core are we a national culture that is fear-based or love-based?
- ➤ How do we measure or define our national spirit?
- ➤ Are we a nation that is based on long-established and predictable laws or a nation based on the presidential personality or whims of the political party currently in power?
- ➤ Are our leaders setting a good example for the rest of us to follow?
- ➤ Are we giving our leaders a clear message of the kind of leadership we want and expect?
- ➤ What is the status of our celebrated freedoms?
- ➤ Is our government functioning to serve the collective needs of the people?
- ➤ Is the president in power above the law?
- ➤ Will there continue to be a peaceful turnover of government in future presidential elections?
- ➤ Do we live up to our promises?
- ➤ Is truth still a core value?
- ➤ Do facts matter?
- ➤ Are we inclined to help each other?
- ➤ Are we open and welcoming?
- ➤ Are we civil to each other, even when we disagree?
- ➤ Are we good stewards of the climate and environment for future generations?
- ➤ Are we fiscally responsible?

- How do we treat our allies?
- How do we treat our adversaries?
- How do we rate as a nation of integrity and adherence to universal values?

Some of the standards that I consider important in answering these questions may not resonate with some of my fellow citizens. That's okay with me because I consider diverse attitudes and opinions to be one of our nation's strengths. My purpose is to stimulate conversation and thoughtful awareness of the collective American consciousness with respect to what we truly value. Is the Trump administration leading us in the right direction?

If we are moving in the wrong direction, how can we reverse course and regain the high ground that many around the world feel the United States held during and after World War II? How do we re-create America as a "shining city on a hill" as described most recently by Ronald Reagan in 1989 during his farewell speech to the nation? What if those same personal attributes for building character in individuals were applied to our nation as a whole? What would a "nation of character" look like? And what will it take to get from here to there?

In the eighteenth century many of the rights and freedoms granted by the Constitution and Bill of Rights were a radical departure from the norm in the nations of Europe from which many of the Founding Fathers were descended. America was new territory and a grand experiment for human rights. In the more than two centuries since the foundation was laid for a nation of character, there have been starts and stops, high points and low points, trials and errors. In this respect, America is a reflection of the journey of its people as well.

The 2016 Election

I believe President Trump was elected for a reason, which may become apparent in the rearview mirror. He may be the painful lesson America needs to learn at this point in its history. Just as Germany may have had to experience the Hitler era, perhaps America had to go through the Trump era. Sometimes we need to experience the darkness of the ego before we can fully appreciate the light.

Our nation was born as a result of independent-minded citizens, strong leadership, and true north principles. Our Founding Fathers were guided by a sense of fairness, equity, justice, integrity, honesty, and trust—as defined by the standards of the time. For America to regain that level of character, we are going to need bold, courageous, honest leadership and an involved citizenry that appreciates the value of integrity, honesty, and fairness for all.

chapter 1

Values

What if the ideals we follow
Lack goodness, truth, and are hollow?
What if power and money
Make our ethics smell funny?
JB

By Definition

Values can be defined as the intangible principles or standards of behavior that are important in life. I think of values as a moral code of conduct. We are naturally drawn to our values, as if they were giant magnets pulling us in their direction. We tend to see the world we value. I believe this is true on an individual basis and as a collective culture. If we value money, deception, and power over honesty, integrity, and respect for one another, we are naturally drawn into a scenario like the current state of politics in Washington, DC. If we value integrity and loving kindness over fear and greed, another and better world emerges from the apparent chaos.

Personally, I have a great appreciation for the traditional American values that have made America stand out as a model for other nations. American values have been the envy of the world. Standards and ideals were growing and developing since before our nation was formed and have dominated the thinking of each subsequent generation. Foreign nations have followed our example. American values have spread to become universal values as well.

Even before the birth of our nation, values were the "stars" that guided ships across the dangerous Atlantic Ocean carrying the first European settlers to America and the promise of religious freedom and opportunities not available to them in Europe. Values guided brave, independent-minded pioneer families westward across a vast and dangerous wilderness, some persevering all the way to the Pacific Ocean in search of a better life. George Washington and his ragged band of soldiers were guided by values as they threw off the yoke of foreign dominion. Values guided our Founding Fathers in creating the US Constitution and the Bill of Rights. Values led President Lincoln and the Union in the fight to end centuries of slavery in America. Values guided our nation to intervene in two world wars to preserve a free and democratic Western civilization. Values persisted in passage of the Civil Rights Act.

American values have been the principles that have guided American leaders and ordinary citizens to be truthful, honest, fair, hard-working, and determined to "do the right thing" even in times of adversity. I see American values as the ideals, the ideas, the motivating factors, the true north principles that have guided America through booms, busts, wars, and peace. Based upon the songs and symbols that represent the United States of America, and a myriad of books and movies defining life in America, there has been general consensus in the past that American values include at least the following concepts:

- ➤ Freedom
- ➤ Equality
- ➤ Opportunity
- ➤ Character
- ➤ Patriotism
- ➤ Truthfulness
- ➤ Decency/respect
- ➤ Civility
- ➤ Fair play
- ➤ Integrity
- ➤ Helping one another
- ➤ Tolerance/diversity
- ➤ Family/community
- ➤ Confidence
- ➤ Education/knowledge
- ➤ Questioning
- ➤ Peace Loving
- ➤ Independent/interdependent
- ➤ Loving kindness
- ➤ Blessed/grateful

These are also basic values that have evolved over time in most of the world's religions, including Christianity, Judaism, Islam, Hindu, and other religious movements over the centuries.

Trumpian Values

Values and character have been hot topics of discussion, especially since the 2016 presidential election. President Donald J. Trump, America's forty-fifth president, who was elected by a minority of American voters, has in a very short time redefined centuries-old American values to reflect his unique, egotistical view of life. During the Trump era American values have come to encompass very different ideals such as:

- ➢ it's all about money and wealth;
- ➢ wealth is the best indicator of intelligence and leadership;
- ➢ the world is made up only of winners and losers;
- ➢ winning is all that matters;
- ➢ lying and cheating are effective tools for winning;
- ➢ diplomacy and economic policies can be used as weapons to force compliance with our wishes;
- ➢ relationships are to be used and are expendable;
- ➢ anger, threats, obstruction, intimidation, and personal attacks are normal business and political practices;
- ➢ personal loyalty to the leader trumps loyalty to America or the Constitution; and
- ➢ power is for bullying and personal enrichment.

The Trump philosophy is clear: if American businesses are profitable; if Trump business enterprises are successful; if the stock market is up; if arms sales to dictators for bombing innocent civilians override international principles of decency; if the president can unilaterally make foreign relations decisions without consulting with Congress, the intelligence community, or our allies; if the president, aided and abetted by Congress, can cut taxes for the rich and cut social safety nets for the poor; if the president only represents and cares about the people who voted for him; if the "base" is like a cult, blindly loyal to its leader; if trillion-dollar deficits in the midst of a booming economy are acceptable; if voter suppression and foreign interference in elections effectively allows Trump and his followers to win elections and stay in power; if science and global warming can be ignored or denied in order to feed corporate greed; if winning elections absolves sinning; if we are winning our trade wars against allies and adversaries; if separating children from their parents is an effective deterrent to requests for asylum from people fleeing violence in Central America; if political power effectively leads to ideological packing of courts; if peaceful civil protesters can be relabeled as "angry mobs"; if truth and facts are irrelevant; if the end justifies the means; if might makes right; and if a critical free press can be misidentified as the "enemy of the state" or "fake news," then American values are flourishing.

The Trump values are about money, power, winning, having unquestioning followers who are blindly loyal, being admired as a stable genius, and bullying anyone who doesn't agree with him, and this is the very nature of his condition. It has always been "all about Trump." Truth, justice, honesty, integrity, and empathy for others are not part of his emotional or mental makeup. He really can't help himself. He is just being himself—the same person he was before becoming president. It is the ultimate responsibility of American voters to elect qualified candidates to office. The buck stops with the American people.

Some members of Congress have enabled this erratic, egotistical president in this quest to redefine our sacred values. Leadership of the Senate has willingly given up its power as a coequal branch of government in order to appease the president. Cowardice, hypocrisy, and greed have largely replaced service, integrity, and independence in the search for votes and money to remain in political office.

So the question for every American citizen ought to be: Am I happy with Trumpian values as long as the economy is good, or do I prefer to move in the direction of traditional American values based on integrity and fair play?

An Ebb and Flow

There has been an ebb and flow of traditional values throughout our history, but there has never been a serious doubt of their survival—until now. There have been times when these stars have shone brightly in a clear sky; there have been times when the stars have been partially blocked by clouds. So far the Trump era has utilized smoke and mirrors, which have dimmed the glow of the stars of American values.

As an American and a citizen of the world, I trust that the stars are still up there, and I sincerely hope that these clouds, too, shall pass. Ultimately, America's future direction will be determined by the collective values and consciousness of the American people—you and me. It is time for each one of us to get to work on defining our own values and ideals. America and the world are depending on us.

chapter 2

Freedom

What if our Founding Fathers
Found freedom to be too much a bother?
What if they focused instead
On feathering their own bed?
Would our guaranteed freedoms be fodder?

JB

Some Americans tend to take for granted the guaranteed freedoms within the Constitution and Bill of Rights. These include the freedom to choose our thoughts, express our ideas, make our own plans, develop our own religious or spiritual beliefs, and follow life's paths wherever they may take us. That is not necessarily the case everywhere in the world, where dictators, social customs, caste systems, and religious dictates allow for limited options. These freedoms represent important American values.

America was settled early on by Europeans, some of whom were actively resisting the authoritarian ways that limited their potentials. They were the malcontents, the rebels, and the mavericks who were willing to question authority and yearned for new freedoms and opportunities. They risked the dangers and unknowns of crossing oceans for the American wilderness. Many of the people who stayed behind made the choice to live out their lives under known but often oppressive conditions.

The America of the twenty-first century consists of a very wide range of individuals and groups. We come in every size, shape, color, religious belief, political persuasion, sexual orientation, level of wealth or poverty, educational background, ethnicity, urbanites and rural, hawks and doves, liberals and conservatives, establishment and outsiders. We come from ancestries that include Indigenous Americans, Europeans, Africans, Latinos, Middle Easterners, and Asians. Our religious portfolio includes Christians, Jews, Muslims, Hindus, Sikhs, Buddhists, Deists, Spiritualists, and Atheists. We are one cultural melting pot, in the process of assimilating as Americans.

Our diversity can be a challenge in everyday life. It can be frustrating for white males in power to have to consider perspectives that are different than their own—from cultures that may be different than the world of white, European descendants in America. That is why protecting our guaranteed freedoms is so important for the ongoing success of the American way for everyone.

Freedom of Religion

Many early Americans came to the New World in the seventeenth and eighteenth centuries to escape religious persecution. Europe was a hotbed of religious fervor, often culminating in a "state religion." Religious wars were European rituals. Anyone not conforming to the religious dictates of the ruling monarch was subject to fines, imprisonment, torture, or worse. England, France, Spain, Italy, and Germany were essentially religious states at times similar to some of today's Muslim countries in the Middle East (Wikipedia). The free pursuit of different religious customs and beliefs was often a dangerous proposition.

Although some early settlers continued to model their behavior after the state religions of Europe, by the end of the eighteenth century freedom of religion had become an accepted norm in America. The Bill of Rights codified the attitude of the people. Separation of church and state became the rule of the land (*Religion in American Politics: A Short History*, by Frank Lambert). This principle has survived and thrived for more than two centuries, freeing all Americans to make their own decisions with regard to religious or spiritual beliefs.

Freedom of religion includes freedom from religion.

Unfortunately clouds have gathered in recent years, narrowing the separation of church and state. With the support and encouragement of President Trump, the Religious Right has taken on the challenge of squelching the rights of "infidels," treating them as an inferior enemy. Religious tolerance is on the ropes in much of America today ("Religious Tolerance in America," the 1a.org). An all-too-common attitude is that "real Americans" are Christian, and that nonbelievers (e.g., Jews, Muslims) do not belong here. Ironically, this attitude is the exact opposite of the teachings of Jesus Christ, the founder of Christianity. It is also opposite the beliefs of many of America's Founding Fathers, some of whom were not practicing Christians.

Personal Experience

I am reminded of my own religious upbringing in rural southern Indiana in the middle of the twentieth century. Everyone who lived in my small town at that time was Catholic and of either German or Swiss ancestry. I was taught by Benedictine nuns and priests in public school that the Roman Catholic Church was the "one true church" and the only way to get to heaven. Daily Mass was a requirement before the start of classes. We were not allowed to visit a Protestant church or befriend a Protestant boy or girl. Marriage between a Catholic and a Protestant was known as a mixed marriage, which resulted in forfeiture of Catholic rights and rites. Jews, Muslims, and other religious groups were simply nonexistent in my childhood experience.

More than sixty years later I can still remember riding my bike home from school and questioning in my mind what I was being taught. The bike was my teaching vehicle from a very early age. The Catholic indoctrination simply made no sense to me, but I did not feel free to question my parents or teachers. Good little boys went along with the program.

Fortunately, I was free to escape this limiting environment as an adult to explore my own religious and spiritual thinking. I was able to form my own opinions without interference from the Catholic Church. That was my American gift of religious freedom, for which I will be forever grateful. I still think of myself as a Christian but also as a person who is willing to question much of the dogma created by religious politicians and rulers over the centuries.

A Christian Nation?

Today organized political pressure is building to once again force religious beliefs onto the masses. Non-Christians are sometimes the victims of violence, treated as unwelcome and second-class citizens. Politicians and far-right thinkers voice the opinion that America is a Christian nation. They would like to replace the American democracy with a Christian theocracy—preferably white. It is the not-so-subtle message behind Trump's political slogan: make America great again.

Powerful forces pushing America in the direction of a white Christian nation can be seen in violent attacks and even the gunning down of Jews and Muslims in synagogues and mosques; in neo-Nazi marches and demonstrations; in governmental policies that deter Muslims from entering America; in Christian sermons by Evangelical preachers pressuring parishioners how to vote in elections; in legislatures diverting public education resources to private Christian schools; and in social media messages spreading fear and hatred of non-Christians ("Americans United for Separation of Church and State," www.au.org).

The Trump administration did not invent this fear and hatred, but they have supported and energized the message from their far-right base, giving aid and comfort to ideas that would have traditionally been considered "Un-American."

Freedom of Speech

Within reasonable limits, Americans have been free to express themselves without regard to the wishes of their fellow citizens or the government. Unpopular opinions have been tolerated as long as they did not represent a danger to other people. People in the United States have been free to be critical of elected officials or political candidates, as evidenced by the smear campaigns routinely involved in election years. However, it is not an acceptable freedom of speech to falsely shout "Fire!" in a crowded theater resulting in mass chaos, deaths, and injuries. Also, untrue defamatory accusations aired against fellow citizens may push the limits of slander or libel laws designed to protect personal reputations. Freedom of speech has its logical limits.

There has been a disturbing attack from the Trump administration on expressed opinions that are critical of the administration's agenda. People who disagree with Trump's words, actions, or policies are routinely ridiculed, shamed, belittled, or bullied—often in the form of "tweets." Peaceful civil protesters can be labeled angry mobs. Professional athletes who courageously call attention to perceived abusive treatment of fellow citizens by kneeling during the pregame National Anthem are called "unpatriotic sons of bitches deserving to be fired." Legitimate freedom of expression is in jeopardy in Trump's America.

It has not been easy, but resistance to Trump has been steady and strong. The free press has been a vital cog in alerting America to the ongoing assault. When the Trump policy was to separate children from their parents who were seeking asylum from violence in their native countries, lawsuits were filed in federal courts and thousands of Americans marched in the streets all over our nation to protest this immoral policy. When law enforcement actions have unfairly targeted minority groups, Black Lives Matter and similar groups have made their voices heard. When the NRA (the "piggy bank" for Trump and Congress) defends the right of hate groups and the mentally unstable to amass unlimited weapons of mass destruction, the media and the American people rise up in protest.

Freedom of the Press

America has a rich history of a free press, dating back to before the Revolutionary War when it rallied the colonists to overthrow British rule. A free press has been a vital instrument in preserving American values through more than two centuries. It regularly calls the government to account for its actions. Journalists are the unsung heroes who protect American values from dangerous, delusional, power-hungry politicians.

There have been numerous examples of what happens in countries without the guarantee of freedom of the press. Journalists have been routinely killed or tortured for expressing opinions that are critical of the ruling government. Such atrocities have occurred in the Middle East, Russia, Central and South America, Southeast Asia, and other places where the media is controlled by the state ("Modern Authoritarianism: Press Freedom," freedomhouse.org). Trump has chosen to cast a blind eye to such atrocities as the apparent torture, murder, and dismemberment of an American resident journalist by Saudi Arabian government leaders. Trump values the financial ties with Saudi Arabia as more important than its government's murderous policies.

Under the Trump administration, journalists critical of his policies and behavior are usually (so far) not physically injured or murdered. Rather, they are bullied, ridiculed, blackballed, and belittled as "fake news," "liars," or the "enemy of the people." There have been some instances when Trump's unstable, cult-like followers have murdered or attempted to attack American journalists. Fortunately, most mentally stable Americans are able to see through his angry tirades and continue to expect the free press to do its job. It is worrisome that Trump and more members of the "Trump cult" might be emboldened to take a more violent approach, similar to that of the government of Saudi Arabia.

Meanwhile, certain elements of the press appear to have sold their souls in order to become the profitable propaganda arm of the administration. Far-right talk show hosts, a certain cable news organization, a major broadcasting company, and others have equated President Trump and his morals to Mother Teresa. Social media is populated by "news" sources that are not always who they appear to be, attempting to influence and obstruct the American democratic system.

Right to Peaceably Assemble

The Women's March on Washington at the time of President Trump's inauguration portended a tumultuous four years for the president. The march has been followed by protest gatherings with every outrageous Trump policy, action, or statement. The streets of America have never been so crowded with citizens' protests. Some protests, such as the marchers across America demanding an end to separation of children from parents at the border, have been largely successful in blocking cruel and inhuman policies. Others, such as the protest over pulling America out of international ecology and arms limitation pacts have had minimal impact on Trump policies.

Movements such as Black Lives Matter and Me Too have used the guaranteed right to peaceably assemble to further their cause for equal justice. Protests over Supreme Court appointments and packing of the federal judicial system have been less successful, but have sent an important message to the administration that voters are watching—as evidenced by results of the midterm elections of 2018.

Ironically, Trump's own political rallies all over the country have sometimes been less than peaceful, as he riles up the crowd to lock up political opponents or violently remove protesters. ("Shocking Supercut Shows," huffpost.com). Trump regularly announces that one political opponent or another is guilty of some crime in his mind and should be "locked up" or "sent back." The constitutional protection of due process apparently does not apply to people who do not agree with Trump. That is a scary change in a traditional American value.

Right to Keep and Bear Arms

America was carved out of the wilderness, and guns were an important tool in battling the elements. Guns proliferated in the "Wild West" for hunting and for protection in the absence of a highly developed military or system of law and order. The gun became a symbol of independence in the American West. The long history of guns in America makes it understandable why the Bill of Rights protected the right to bear arms.

The emotional connection to guns is very high in America compared to most countries in Europe and around the world. There are many millions of guns in the possession of a large segment of American society. As a consequence, America has suffered the pains of an extremely high number of deaths and injuries due to gunshots. Mass shootings have become an almost everyday occurrence. Military-style assault rifles are readily available to the general public and have been an effective tool for mentally unstable killers to use in civilian massacres.

The Second Amendment has been a "hot potato" in an America that continues to experience mass shootings on a routine daily basis. The defensive position of the powerful gun lobbying group—the National Rifle Association—has been that no limits should be placed on the rights of citizens to assemble arsenals of weapons. Military-style assault rifles are perfectly acceptable in the hands of mentally unstable individuals and groups, regardless of the mass shooting deaths of elementary, high school, and university students ("How the NRA Rewrote the Second Amendment," brennancenter. org). The position of the NRA and its pocketed politicians is the moral equivalent of defending the right to falsely shout "Fire!" in a crowded theater as freedom of expression. The NRA has spent unlimited funds to lobby representatives of all branches of government, thereby successfully maintaining legal protections over the arms industry and its customers.

President Trump has been a consistent proponent of the NRA and an unfettered Second Amendment. It appears that the political and financial backing of this organization is of greater "value" than the lives of the shooting victims and their families.

chapter 3

Equality

What if the color of skin
Or one's national origin
Were simply nonissues
With no need for tissues
To wipe away decades of sin?
JB

Equal Justice

Constitutional guarantees would be worthless without independent courts to protect them. Article III of the Constitution was designed to provide a system of justice for all Americans. The federal judiciary is protected from the influence of the other two branches of government, allowing judges to make decisions based on what is right under the law, without political consequences.

Etched in stone above the main entrance to the United States Supreme Court are these words: EQUAL JUSTICE UNDER LAW. Equal justice in the judicial system is a promise to all Americans. It is a concept that is a cornerstone of life in America. When equal justice is missing, all Americans suffer the consequences. Equality is one of America's most valued ideals.

Equal justice means that all Americans have the same opportunity to succeed; that everyone has equal access to quality and affordable education; that all persons, regardless of religious beliefs, color of skin, ethnic origin, or sexual orientation, are treated the same by law enforcement officials; that judicial sentencing guidelines for convicted criminals are applied uniformly and fairly regardless of the race or ethnicity of the convict; that governmental policies and practices are designed to protect all of its citizens from discrimination and bigotry; and that everyone has equal access to job opportunities with equal pay for equal work.

An Inconsistent History

There have been unfortunate periods in American history when equal justice failed to materialize. In the nineteenth century Native Americans were forced to give up their ancestral lands to make way for European settlers, leaving only a "trail of tears" as the survivors trekked westward to unforgiving wilderness reservations ("The Story of the Trail of Tears," kawvalley.k12.ks.us). African Americans endured centuries of slavery, followed by a century and a half (so far) of segregation, discrimination, second-class educations, voter suppression, and violence at the hands of white mobs and sometimes law enforcement officials ("Black Americans Victims of Hate Crimes," texastribune.org). Chinese Americans were exploited for labor as railroads expanded westward (*Building the Transcontinental Railroad,* History Channel). Japanese Americans were interned in prison camps and some of their assets confiscated during World War II (*Japanese Internment Camps,* History Channel). Women waited until the twentieth century to get the right to vote, and continue to receive unequal pay and unequal employment opportunities.

Racial profiling continues to be an unofficial police strategy in much of America today, with African Americans, Native Americans, Asian Americans, and Latinos bearing the brunt of racial profiling and violence perpetrated in the name of law enforcement.

Notwithstanding these glaring blemishes on American history, equal justice under the law remains an important American ideal. Substantial progress has been made in recent decades, with passage of the Nineteenth Amendment to the Constitution giving women the right to vote, the Civil Rights Act, the Americans with Disabilities Act, and important court decisions that have gone a long way toward providing a framework of equal protection and equal justice for all Americans.

The Trump Record on Equality

Equal justice has not been a priority for the Trump administration. Policies have been established without regard to laws or tradition. When courts have ruled against him or his policies based on the laws of the land, he has attacked the impartial judiciary as partisan "Obama judges" or "Clinton judges." He has denigrated the neutrality of federal judges like Judge Curiel, an American with Hispanic roots, who issued a ruling that was unfavorable to the now-defunct Trump University (CNN.com).

Trump nominated Jeff Sessions as attorney general and head of the Justice Department because he thought Sessions would be personally loyal to him rather than to the attorney general's constitutional duties, and without regard to his past that included racial discrimination issues. When Sessions properly followed well established law and recused himself from overseeing the independent counsel's investigation of Trump's possible Russian connections and obstruction of justice, Trump whined, complained, ridiculed, and eventually fired him. He replaced Sessions with Bill Barr, who appears to be only too happy to be Trump's toady attorney general (politico.com).

Immigration policies under the Trump administration have been slanted in favor of white Christians and against persons of color, Muslims, or anyone else who does "not look like us and may not vote with us." The melting pot appears to be undergoing a purification process alarmingly similar to the Nazi Germany experience almost a century ago.

John Adams, a Founding Father of our great nation, indicated that America is "a government of laws, not men." Trump has demonstrated an authoritarian disrespect for the rule of law, intimating that because he is president he is above the law rather than being subject to it—like the rest of us ordinary citizens. His obnoxious, abusive, obstructive behavior has become the "new normal" (*Trump's Assault on the Rule of Law*, Robert Reich).

It is no wonder that Trump's most admired world leaders are authoritarian strongmen in the Middle East, Russia, China, and North Korea. These are men who are assured complete political power for their lifetimes. It has caused concerned Americans to wonder if Trump would willingly and peacefully turn over governmental power to a political opponent if he is voted out of office in 2020 elections.

I trust that enlightened and fair-minded Americans are in favor of the concept and the practice of equal justice under law, applicable to everyone. I would like to believe that many of the neo-Nazis, white supremacists, white nationalists, and other ignorant and bigoted groups that have come out of hiding during the Trump era will lose their influence on societal values when Trump finally passes from the political scene.

chapter 4

Opportunity

What if the American dream
Is a boost to our national esteem?
Available to all
To rise or to fall
As one, or as part of the team.
JB

The Land of Opportunity

Many immigrants were drawn to our shores with the belief that the American dream was real and unlimited. Hard work and honest effort could result in successes out of reach in their native lands. The American experience indicates that the dream is true; there are no barriers or limits to success in America—just obstacles to overcome with intelligence, hard work, and a willingness to take risk. Immigrants populate some of the most successful ranks in the nation.

These opportunity-driven immigrants arrived from Europe, Asia, and Central and South America. Pioneers settled the Midwest and West during much of the nineteenth century. Life was challenging, but land was cheap.

Immigrants from Africa were not as fortunate, as they were brought to this country against their will and enslaved for cheap labor. It should not be surprising that this group of immigrants has so far been less successful in taking full advantage of the land of opportunity.

Through the hard work of generations, America has been dramatically transformed from a wilderness that stretched forever to a civilization of farmers, ranchers, business owners, factory workers, builders, railroad workers, truck drivers, grocery stores, saloons, prospectors, educators, clergy, bankers, brewers, vintners, soldiers, law enforcement officials, and outlaws. There are limitless ways to succeed in America, and many Americans have followed their dreams. Opportunity has been a valuable principle in America's history.

The entrepreneurial spirit has thrived in America from the very beginning, with a freedom to succeed or fail in a free enterprise system that has been unmatched in the history of the world. Fortunes have been made, lost, and sometimes frittered away by subsequent generations. Fortunes have come from the land, mining, animal furs, trading, gambling, beer and wine, construction, housing, transportation, petroleum, professional services, criminal enterprises, and every conceivable want or need of the population.

Immigrants have pursued the American dream with a sense of freedom to use their talents to farm, start businesses, become professionals, develop specialty restaurants and foods, or utilize their experience as carpenters, tradesmen, bankers, brewers, or clothiers ("Six Amazing Immigrant Entrepreneurs," smallbiztrends.com).

Inventors such as Thomas Edison and manufacturers such as Henry Ford thrived in an America that provided the economic climate, legal system, workforce, and political stability for success. More recently America has been a haven for developing high-tech companies that are dominating and changing the world economy. American ingenuity is valued everywhere and is copied by companies around the world.

Major universities were founded early and often in the American experience, providing scholars and scientists with educational opportunities previously limited to the elite classes. These universities have become magnets for students from around the world, many of whom want to remain in America to pursue their careers long after formal education is complete.

The Trump Version of Opportunity

President Trump has demonstrated a slightly different approach to business entrepreneurship than the American norm. He appears to view the land of opportunity as an opportunity to treat people badly. Early in his career, with a family fortune in his pocket, it is reported that he routinely "stiffed" subcontractors, plumbers, electricians, attorneys, bankers, architects, engineers, and anyone else he could bully in order to increase his personal wealth ("Donald Trump's Business Plan Left a Trail of Unpaid Bills," wsj.com). The federal bankruptcy laws and court system were just weapons in his arsenal when his business ventures did not perform up to his expectations.

He reportedly discriminated against minority groups in his housing practices, and then, with the help of his subsequently disbarred attorney Roy Kohn, bullied the federal government into settling his legal violations ("Trump and His Father were Sued for Racial Discrimination," *Newsweek*). If the reports are accurate, his was a business legacy of shady practices and broken promises ("Trump's Long War with Justice," politico).

As president, the Trump era has imposed severe limits on who is welcome in America ("Muslim Ban," Executive Order 13769). Some of the immigrants who helped to build our great nation are now being deported, with families torn apart. Trump has ordered ICE to conduct raids to remove undocumented immigrants. Over a million people face removal orders, with separation of parents from children an inevitable consequence (CNN Politics). Foreign technology specialists, researchers, and scientists who are desperately needed by American technology firms are often not welcomed into our country. Asylum seekers from Central America who are ready, willing, able, and eager to perform the dirty, difficult tasks that many Americans are unwilling to do have been detained, arrested, and sent back to their violent native countries.

Ironically, it appears that Trump companies have illegally benefited from hiring undocumented foreign workers at his own resorts and other business establishments (motherjones. com). The opportunity for cheap labor has its place in the Trump world.

Tax laws have been passed during the Trump era to favor super-rich business owners while suppressing the economic plight of workers. Too often workers must put in long hours at multiple jobs in order to eke out a living, thereby limiting the opportunity to pursue their own business or educational dreams.

Growth Opportunities

In addition to being a land of business and financial opportunities, America has provided a climate for personal growth, allowing its people such basic freedoms as choosing: whom or whether to marry, whether or not to be a part of a religious group, among myriad fields of education or technical training, career paths, where and how to live, sexual orientation, and personal health-care decisions. These opportunities, too, have been under assault during Trump's time as president. Education has become less affordable, thereby putting a damper on educational aspirations; desperately needed money has been diverted from the public school system to Christian-based or for-profit institutions, which often under serve the working poor and minorities; federal courts have been packed with judges ideologically prone to suppress personal choices; consumer and environmental protections from abuse by powerful financial and business industries have been undermined; and affordable health care for average Americans has been made less available.

chapter 5

Character

What if victory is fleeting,
If winning involves cheating?
What if veracity counts,
Whether in a losing effort or trounce?
JB

Character can be defined as the sum total of our personality. A person of character is the result of a continuing effort to "do the right thing," choosing thoughts and actions that are strong, confident, kind, loving, helpful, and positive.

Building Blocks

Some of the building blocks of character that I discuss in my second book, *Character Building,* include:

- ➢ authenticity, being real and genuine;
- ➢ awareness and appreciation of our many blessings;
- ➢ commitment to thoughts and ideals that are greater than ourselves;
- ➢ caring for and respecting one another;

- ➢ a positive attitude and determination to overcome difficult challenges;
- ➢ empathy for others;
- ➢ understanding and forgiveness;
- ➢ faith, with an inner knowing that everyone we meet is also a spiritual being sharing this human journey with us;
- ➢ a generous, giving attitude;
- ➢ grace and calmness under pressure;
- ➢ unpretentious with genuine humility;
- ➢ honesty and integrity;
- ➢ basic fairness and sense of justice;
- ➢ having respect for the truth;
- ➢ being of service;
- ➢ having a clear mission and purpose in life;
- ➢ a friendly, neighborly attitude;
- ➢ open-mindedness;
- ➢ bold, daring, unafraid; and
- ➢ warm, welcoming, and helpful.

Character is damaged by such attitudes and practices as:

- ➢ being physically or emotionally abusive;
- ➢ self-absorbed, egotistical, or narcissistic actions;
- ➢ bullying the weak or vulnerable;
- ➢ bigotry and racism;
- ➢ lying and cheating;
- ➢ fear and defensiveness;
- ➢ whining and complaining;
- ➢ being hypocritical;
- ➢ spreading hate;
- ➢ acting like an obnoxious jerk;
- ➢ mean-spirited attacks;

> ➤ intentionally and maliciously inflicting harm on a person or other living thing;
> ➤ cruel sarcasm or belittling another person;
> ➤ self centeredness with total lack of empathy;
> ➤ unethical, lacking basic moral principles;
> ➤ vanity and pretentiousness; and
> ➤ with illusions of grandeur.

The recent death of our forty-first president, George Herbert Walker Bush, was a reawakening to the importance of character in American government. Although his policies were not always universally appreciated, the character of President Bush was seldom at issue. His long record of military and public service contrasts sharply with the Trump record. Bush was widely remembered for being a decent human being with a relatively high degree of character for an American president.

As described in my second book, *Character Building*, people of character have a moral compass that points true north. They are honest, trustworthy, dependable, steadfast, strong, and committed to doing the right thing. They tell the truth, even when the truth is inconvenient. That is essentially how President Bush was remembered by a grateful nation.

The stark contrast between President Bush and President Trump was not-so-subtly evident in eulogies, editorials, and commentary from world leaders around the globe ("Praise for President Bush unavoidably contained critiques of Trump," desmoineregister.com). The contrast was so evident that President Trump was present but excluded from the funeral process, even though former presidents of the opposing party were welcomed and invited to participate ("Trump could've ruined Bush's funeral. Bush didn't let him," washingtonpost.com).

It has been widely recognized that character is sadly missing in the Trump administration, and its absence is having a negative impact on all Americans, from Congress to a frustrated electorate. The example of a leader totally lacking in character has deepened the divide in America, as Trump loyalists (the shrinking base) dig in to defend him no matter what, and the rest of America and the world shake their collective heads in wonder at Trump-style behavior.

Demonstrations of Character

It took character for Abraham Lincoln to unite a nation divided by slavery; it took character for the people of the United States and their sons and daughters to intervene in two world wars; it took character to march in Selma, Alabama, and to pass the Civil Rights Act to protect an oppressed segment of citizens; it took character to protest and ultimately force an end to the Vietnam War. American character has been demonstrated by leaders and by ordinary citizens. An abundance of character has been evident throughout American history.

Character Building identifies some of the historical role models possessing strong, deep character. People such as George Washington, John Adams, Abe Lincoln, Franklin D. Roosevelt, Winston Churchill, Margaret Thatcher, Dr. Martin Luther King Jr., Mother Teresa, and Gandhi have demonstrated their depth and strength of character on the world stage. President Trump is likely to go down in history as "a character" but not as "a person of character."

Unfathomable harm has been done to America's collective consciousness during the Trump era, and it will require a future president with depth and strength of character to lead America on a new and higher path.

chapter 6

Patriotism

What if love of one's nation
Involves more than a tough attitude?
But includes in the equation
A helpful, caring mood?

JB

The Meaning of Patriotism

Rarely has a word been so misconstrued and misunderstood as patriotism. Traditionally, patriotism has meant a love of one's country, an emotional attachment to our nation, a spirit of support and defense of our nation's ideals, and a willingness to defend our sovereignty and our way of life. It has never been about winning a competition by beating down everyone else by intimidation and bullying. It is not necessarily patriotic to go to war.

As an elementary school student in Ferdinand, Indiana, more than sixty-five years ago, I stood facing the American flag and proudly recited the Pledge of Allegiance every morning. My memory is that it was a pledge not just to our flag but to the nation the flag represented—the American people and

American values. My personal thoughts were on equality, liberty, and justice for all. For me there was no military or violent aspect to the pledge.

Patriotism is not exclusively a military term. Clearly, our dedicated military men and women are patriots. We owe them a tremendous debt of gratitude for protecting our nation and our ideals from foreign adversaries who may intend us harm. We honor their service and owe them a functional medical care system for their physical, mental, and emotional needs during and after service.

In addition to the military, patriots live among the law-abiding civilian population in the form of school teachers, professors, students, nurses, medical doctors, newspaper editors, journalists, firefighters, law enforcement officials, celebrities, athletes, farmers, attorneys, judges, accountants, civil servants, priests, ministers, rabbis, retirees, volunteers, business owners, executives, construction workers, librarians, musicians, entertainers, authors, engineers, social workers, automobile assemblers, scientists, local government officials, bartenders, servers, mental health professionals, computer technicians, and every other way of life that supports and promotes our nation's cherished values.

School Spirit

I am reminded of a lesson I learned in high school about sixty years ago. Some teenagers back then equated "school spirit" (akin to patriotism) to being an athlete (akin to warrior), participating in macho sports such as basketball and football that represented the school in competitions with other schools. The non-athletes such as yearbook staffers, school newspaper reporters, actors in school plays, orchestra members, debaters, cheerleaders, or top students were not perceived as having the same level of school spirit as these athletes. They were simply not equal to the warrior class.

I argued then, and still believe today, that patriots come in many forms, shapes, colors, and sizes. Warriors and athletes do not own the concept. Sometimes protestors of immoral practices are the true patriots. Sometimes just being helpful to someone in need is patriotism in action.

Nationalism or Patriotism?

Nationalism is sometimes confused with patriotism. Although there are some similarities in their meanings, nationalism has an exclusionary element, putting national or ideological interests above the needs of others. Patriots believe in the goodness of their country, its government, and fellow citizens, all working together for the welfare of the country. Nationalists believe their country is superior to all other countries (thoughtco.com).

Nationalism may favor strong borders to keep out "undesirables", winning at the expense of our allies, using military-style tactics to suppress the rights of groups with opposing views, valuing symbolism (the flag, national anthem, military parades, fireworks, saluting) over basic kindness and recognizing the reality of inequality and social injustice. In the Trump era it has come to mean political movements such as neo-Nazis, white nationalism, and white supremacy. In this sense, nationalism is the opposite of patriotism. It divides our citizens rather than uniting us for the common good of our nation and the world.

Nationalism may include symbolically saluting the American flag and standing for the National Anthem, but it does not always support and promote America's most cherished values. Often it goes against the grain of traditional values.

Until the American people fully accept, understand, and appreciate the difference between the true spirit of patriotism and patriotic symbols, we will remain a divided nation permeated by fear and anger.

Trump and Patriotism

As a young man of privilege, Trump declined the opportunity to serve his country in military service. Bone spurs diagnosed by a friendly podiatrist allegedly renting office space from Trump's father entitled Donald to be exempted from service. *Trump made up injury to dodge Vietnam service, his former lawyer Michael Cohen testifies, in Senate Intelligence Committee Hearing.* His Vietnam experience was spent enjoying New York City's social life, dodging sexually transmitted diseases, playing golf, and increasing his family's fortune.

As president, Trump claims to "know more than the generals" and enjoys surrounding himself with military heroes, unless the real heroes like John McCain disagree with him. He loves military-style parades full of pomp and ceremony, with lots of saluting, fireworks, flyovers, and military equipment. He seems to have conveniently forgotten his personal record as a draft dodger.

chapter 7

Truthfulness

What if a lack of deceit
Was required for a Senate seat?
What if the commander in chief
Had to prove he's no cheat?
JB

The Foundation

Truth is a fundamental American value. In the absence of truth, there cannot be trust. When political leaders disdain the truth, the citizenry and the world become skeptical and rebellious. Truth is the foundation for a stable government. Lack of regard for the truth is a major factor in the current turmoil in American government.

Former Secretary of State Rex Tillerson, himself a casualty of the Trump administration, put it this way: "If our leaders seek to conceal the truth or we as people become accepting of alternate realities that are no longer grounded in facts, then we as American citizens are on a pathway to relinquishing our freedom. This is the life of nondemocratic societies, comprised of people who are not free to seek the truth" (robesonian.com).

Almost every child in America has been taught the importance of telling the truth. America has a long history from George Washington who "could not tell a lie" to "Honest Abe" Lincoln. Telling the truth has been an honored tradition in America for centuries. Truth matters in our culture—especially truth from our governmental leaders, who are expected to set examples for all Americans to follow. Truth is an essential American value.

Not every US president has lived up to the high standards set by President Washington and President Lincoln, but successful and revered occupants of the Oval Office have made a genuine effort to be reasonably transparent and basically truthful to the American people. They have not intentionally abused the traditional values of honesty and truthfulness on a routine, daily basis.

An Absence of Truth

There are liars who lie in order to mislead or gain an advantage over others. Although not an admirable trait, there is some logic to such lies. Then there are compulsive liars and pathological liars who feel compelled to lie about almost everything, regardless of the situation. They just make things up. This type of untruth makes no logical sense. It is an indication of a personality disorder.

Perhaps more than any other value, truthfulness has been most absent in the Trump era. A day does not pass without knowingly false statements, half-truths, or outrageous and misleading comments. Trump often appears to contradict his own lies, like a criminal who isn't smart enough to keep his alibis straight. This habitual lying has destroyed any semblance of trust in what he says. After years of lies, only the most gullible members of his shrinking base actually believe what he says. He has earned the "Bottomless Pinocchios" awarded to him on a regular basis by the free press ("Washington Post fact-checker introduces 'Bottomless Pinocchio' rating to call Trump on repeated false claims," thehill.com).

When a person lies without demonstrating any sense of shame, it is an unsettling experience for the people aware of the lies. Americans have been taught to associate being dishonest with feeling ashamed or guilty ("Lying, Guilt, and Shame," aeaweb.org). When a conscience is missing, there are no boundaries to violating the truth—especially for someone who considers himself above the law. Such appears to be the case with our president.

The Mueller report exposes a code of conduct in the Trump administration that is focused on covering up and protecting the president from criminal charges or impeachment. Placing pressure on underlings to lie to investigators is apparently standard operating procedure. The goal, always, is to hide or "spin" the dubious intentions and radical behavior of the president of the United States.

Lies Have Consequences

As an honest role model for American children and adults, President Trump has failed miserably. As an image of a trustworthy president, Trump has failed with intelligent, rational, open-minded American voters. Foreign leaders have learned to ignore the words of the American president, much as Western leaders learned to disbelieve the words of Adolf Hitler before and during World War II.

The total absence of truth in the Trump administration has put the American democratic system in moral jeopardy.

Moral leadership of the free world has been squandered. America's image in the world as a shining star has been reduced to a cruel joke.

Reactions from Conservatives

Jan and I live in Southwest Florida, a land of retirees who tend to be politically conservative. Many of our friends and golfing buddies are former business owners or professionals who appreciate Trump's policies of lower taxes, smaller government, and less government regulation of businesses. Interestingly, when asked how they feel about Trump as a person, the most common descriptions from this loyal voting base include the terms "liar" and "idiot."

chapter 8

Decency/Respect

What if instead of being a jerk,
Our president just went to work
Leaving tweeting aside,
The common good as his guide,
Instead of going berserk?
JB

Common Decency

Most people have a sense of what is meant by common decency. Personally, I think the term simply means not acting like an "a--hole." It includes a willingness to conform to societal standards of taste and behavior, with respect for others even in the face of competition or disagreement. The absence of common decency inevitably leads to chaos, fear, rage, violence, and turmoil.

Trump has violated every principle of common decency in his egotistical, narcissistic approach to life and the presidency. Lying, cheating, bullying, name-calling, and fits of anger are beneath the dignity of most adult Americans. They are beneath the dignity of most juveniles as well. To observe this behavior coming from the president of the United States is more than disturbing. America is now paying the price for the lack of common decency within the top levels of government, and civilizations all over the world are watching as this traditional American value crumbles.

Respect

It has been an American ideal to respect the rights and traditions of other people. Mutual respect has been a key to the strong relationships formed by the United States with allies around the globe. Mutual respect has also made it possible for America to become a melting pot of diversity. Respect means that we practice tolerance, consider the feelings of others, and avoid intentionally hurting or belittling other people. Respect means not mocking physically disabled persons.

The feeling of respect for others begins with self-respect. We can't give something that we don't have inside of us. Many mental-health professionals believe that therein lies the problem with our current president.

Disrespect for Legitimate and Important Institutions

Decades, and in some cases centuries, have gone into the creation and evolution of American institutions that serve the vital interests of our citizens and the world. They have earned the respect of almost everyone. In a matter of less than one term in public office, President Trump has diminished the reputations and authority of many of these institutions.

> ➢ The federal judiciary has been the impartial, unbiased interpreter of the laws of the land for more than two centuries. The system has not been flawless, but it has

been impressive in its apolitical efforts to maintain a "nation of laws, not of men." It has provided stability and predictability in the face of difficult challenges. The federal judiciary is perhaps the most vital cog in the American system of justice for all. It is a national treasure to be revered, respected, and defended from ignorant or self-serving politicians.

When Trump did not get a favorable decision involving the now defunct Trump University, he blamed it on a "biased Mexican judge" because Judge Muriel's ancestors had immigrated to America from Mexico. When federal courts regularly overrule his immoral and unconstitutional policies involving immigration, he blames it on "Clinton judges" or "Obama judges." It has been such a disgraceful and destructive attitude that Chief Justice Roberts, a "Bush judge" by Trump's standards, has had to remind Trump on more than one occasion that federal judges are impartial and unbiased, no matter who appointed them to the bench ("In rare rebuke, Chief Justice Roberts shames Trump," NBC News).

> The mission of the Department of Justice is: "To administer an efficient and responsive justice system. Invest in and develop people, processes and technology to ensure continued compliance with legislative and regulatory requirements and sustained public confidence."

Justice has the awesome responsibility to enforce the laws of the land, to defend the interests of the United States according to law, to protect against both foreign and domestic threats, to seek just punishment for those guilty of unlawful behavior, and to ensure fair and impartial administrative justice for all Americans. The Justice Department has been a highly respected institution.

The Mueller investigation of the Trump campaign's possible involvement with Russia to rig the 2016 election, and to determine if the president had obstructed justice in his efforts to thwart the ongoing investigation, was an operation within the Justice Department. Rather than allowing the justice system to operate independently, Trump first demanded that "his" Attorney General Jeff Sessions remain in control of the investigation despite conflicts of interest. When Trump failed in this effort, he debased the investigation as a "hoax" or "witch hunt" literally hundreds of times. In the process, he debased the reputation and standing of the Justice Department.

Nowhere in the laws, regulations, or policies of the Justice Department is it stated that the nation's Justice Department is the personal law firm of the president of the United States. Trump seems to think that the US Department of Justice and the nation's attorney general are his new version of Roy Kohn and Michael Cohen (both disbarred following their years of overzealous representation of Trump), in existence only to protect and further his personal interests. Newly appointed Attorney General William Barr, however, is affirming Trump's belief that the attorney general is "his personal attorney" ("Duties of the Attorney General are to represent the United States in legal matters," justice.gov).

> Likewise, the Federal Bureau of Investigation is intended to defend and protect the United States and to uphold and enforce its criminal laws. The FBI is a branch within the Justice Department. It is not a political arm of the executive branch, intended to protect the president from investigation for wrongdoing.

When FBI Director James Comey declined to offer his personal loyalty to Trump (eerily similar to the Hitler approach of requiring a pledge of absolute personal loyalty to "Der Fuhrer"), and Comey declined Trump's request to "go easy" on Michael Flynn, he was fired as director of the FBI. Comey's firing was followed up with irrational claims of Comey's corruption, incompetence, and bias—all fabrications from a twisted mind. Trump's more recent attacks on top officials of the FBI and Justice Department have included the term "treason" ("Trump, not understanding treason, names people he thinks committed the crime," washingtonpost. com). The damage done to the reputation of these vital institutions by Trump's baseless accusations may take decades to repair.

> ➢ The North Atlantic Treaty Organization (NATO) has been an effective alliance of nations that has maintained a relatively peaceful world following World War II. It has protected Western Europe from the menace of the former Soviet Union, and now Russia. By protecting Western Europe, it has indirectly but surely provided a buffer zone to protect America. NATO remains a vital cog in maintaining peace in the world. America's longtime allies in Europe are dependent on NATO's continuing existence and strength.

Trump has undermined the value and credibility of NATO to the chagrin of foreign leaders and most members of Congress, and to the delight of Putin and Russia. For Trump, it is "all about money." He fails to understand or care about the underlying mission of the organization ("Trump opens NATO Summit with blistering attack on allies," cnn.com).

> ➤ The news media has played an important role in educating and informing the American people on business and political issues in America and the world. Having a free press is a tremendous asset for our nation. Journalists have been instrumental in holding politicians and public figures accountable for their actions. Journalists were instrumental in bringing down the dishonest and corrupt Nixon administration. Trump has good reason to fear an independent, free press.

Hardly a day goes by without tweets or comments by Trump about "fake news," "the failing New York Times," "fake news CNN," or calling the free press "enemies of the people" ("Trump ramps up rhetoric on media," thechill.com). Trump seems determined to eliminate an independent, free press and replace it with "state-controlled" sources of news ala Mr. Putin.

> ➤ The Environmental Protection Agency was established in 1970 during the Nixon administration to protect human health and the environment. It has played a leadership role in working with state and local governments and other nations to protect the global environment.

The EPA is supposed to ensure that: "Americans have clean air, land, and water; utilize best available scientific information to reduce environmental risks; contaminated and toxic sites are to be cleaned up and revitalized; and it makes sure that America is a good steward of the environment and our natural resources." Over nearly five decades, it has been instrumental in policies limiting carbon emissions, including a manyfold increase in vehicle mileage resulting in lower emissions and less consumption of oil and gas.

Trump has undermined the efforts of the EPA by placing at its helm political appointees having a track record of wanting to do away with the agency or having strong ties to the coal industry, which is one of the largest sources of air, land, and water pollution. Protective regulations to the environment have been dismantled or rolled back in order to increase the bottom line for big corporations. The EPA is a casualty of Trump politics ("Who's running Trump's EPA?" environmentalintegrity.org).

> ➤ The Federal Reserve Board is the central banking system of our nation. For more than a century it has had control of the monetary system in order to alleviate financial crises. The Fed Board is appointed by the president, subject to confirmation by the Senate. It is intended to operate independently from politics. The Fed relies on economic expertise rather than political pressure when making its decisions on money supply and interest rates.

President Trump has been attempting to intimidate the Federal Reserve Board of Governors into making interest rate decisions based on Trump's political whims and financial benefits ("A New Tactic in Trump's War on the Fed. He can't fire Powell, so he's sending over dreadful nominees to make the chairman's job harder," wsj.com). He has proposed new members of the Board of Governors who have neither the economic expertise nor experience for the job, although they do have political connections with Trump. It is just another example of debasing this important American agency for his political gain.

> ➤ The United States intelligence community consists of seventeen separate agencies under the coordination of the Office of the Director of National Intelligence. They conduct intelligence activities to support the foreign policy and national security of the United States. The intelligence community as a whole has nearly a million workers with top-security clearances.

President Trump routinely discounts the advice of the people who have spent their careers keeping America safe. He prefers to make his own "seat of the pants" decisions based on his "gut." To their credit, the directors of these agencies have made it clear in testimony before Congress that the facts often disagree with the president's gut decisions ("Testimony by intelligence chiefs on global threats highlight differences with president," *Washington Post*).

> ➤ The executive branch of government is the closest that America comes to royalty. Presidents and their families live in the White House attended by a legion of servants and aides. The president wields almost king-like powers, heavily influencing the military, Congress, intelligence, budget issues, taxation, judicial appointments, cabinet positions, and generally overseeing the activities of the governmental bureaucracy, including the Justice Department and various federal agencies. Serving as president of the United States is a huge responsibility, often described as the most powerful position in the world.

According to the Mueller report, the executive branch under Trump's guidance has been chaotic, deceiving, and threatening. He has used the powers of the presidency to manipulate the Justice Department, including the FBI. In plain sight he has established a revolving door of political appointments to high-level positions with no credentials or experience other than wealth and money. Spokespersons for the president have been coerced into deceiving the American people. He has forever cheapened the office of the president.

Insults and Nicknames

Violations of standards of common decency are demonstrated daily in so many ways that would make a seventh-grader cringe:

➢ by Trump disrespecting his fellow Republican can-didates during the 2016 campaign, referring to them as "Low Energy Jeb," "Lyin' Ted," "Little Marco," etc.;

➢ the draft dodger in chief stooped to a new low when he belittled the heroic military record of Senator John McCain, insinuating that he was a "loser" because he was captured, imprisoned, and tortured by the Viet Cong;

➢ by disrespecting his political adversaries, dubbing them "Crooked Hillary," "Pocahontas," "Crazy Bernie," "Cryin' Chuck," "Nervous Nancy," "Liddle Bob," "Crazy Maxine, "Horseface," "Slime Ball Jim," "Da Nang Dick," "Little Adam Schitt," "Jeff Bozo," "Fatty Nadler," "Sneaky Dianne," "Low IQ Joe," "Lightweight Loser Amash"; "Wacky Jacky," "Dumb as a Box of Rocks Rex," "Fake News CNN"; and "Failing New York Times"; et al;

➢ by referring to lesser developed nations in Africa and Central America as "s---hole" countries;

➤ by debasing foreign leaders ("Little Rocket Man"); insulting our strongest ally, Canada's Justin Trudeau, calling him "dishonest and weak"; calling London Mayor Khan a "stone cold loser," etc.;

➤ by pretentious claims about his wealth, intelligence, scholastic record (conveniently hidden from view), golfing ability, sole power to fix the world's problems, taking personal credit for a rising stock market, calling himself a "stable genius"; and,

➤ by belittling and debasing anyone who expresses disagreement with his opinions or policies.

Time to Heal

Never has there been a clearer case for the need for respect and common decency in government, politics, and life. America and the world have witnessed firsthand the juvenile behavior coming from arguably the most powerful position on earth. The anger, turmoil, divisiveness, and chaos that have ensued should come as no surprise. The behavior goes against the grain of the teachings of civilized society, Christianity, and most other recognized religions. The Dark Ages have gone on too long. It is time to turn away from the darkness and toward the light. Our way of life and traditional American values depend on it.

Other nations are reluctantly stepping forward to pick up the slack during the Trump era. It remains to be seen if America can reclaim its world leadership position when the "Trump dust" settles.

chapter 9

Civility

What if just being nice
In our words and our deeds would suffice
To improve all our lives
As higher nature revives?
A better world at such a small price!

JB

Civility

There is a correlation between civilization and civility. A civilized world is one in which people are civil to one another. We demonstrate civility when we are friendly and nice to another person—whether that person is family, friend, stranger, or competitor. In many civilized social circles in America, civility is the norm. It is a traditional American value to be friendly and nice. It is what we expect of ourselves, and it is what we expect of other people in our daily lives.

Merriam-Webster defines civility as "polite, reasonable, and respectful behavior." The Institute for Civility in Government goes further, indicating that "civility is disagreeing without disrespect, and seeking common ground for dialogue about differences."

According to Jeb Bush, one of Trump's competitors for the Republican presidential nomination in 2016, "Treating people fairly and with civility is not a bad thing. It would be good for our country if political leaders actually took that to heart." His comments were a prophetic warning of what was to come after the election.

The 2016 presidential election shined a light on the lack of civility, including name-calling and bullying. According to the National Council of State Legislatures, 70 percent of respondents to a recent survey believe that incivility in the United States has risen to crisis levels.

Acting with civility appears to be unnatural for this president. His natural tendency is to be defensive, angry, belittling others, and name-calling to help him feel better about himself—unless he is trying to sell something to the other person. It is the kind of behavior we would expect from a Mafia don.

Unfortunately, his style of behavior has spread. It has infected Trump's spokespersons, some of whom follow his example and treat the media with lies, incivility, anger, and disdain. It has also spread to Congress, with some of his supporters resorting to incivility in dealing with their fellow members of Congress and the media. Incivility is like a virus that is infecting the American people.

Trump's Record

Many mental health professionals subscribe to a psychological theory called "projection." The thinking is that projection is a defensive mechanism in which unwanted feelings about our self are subconsciously denied and then projected out onto someone else. If we subconsciously lack basic self-respect and self-esteem, it is unlikely that we will respect and esteem others. If we know deep down that we are dishonest liars or thieves, it is likely that we will attach that description to other people. If we don't feel very smart, we will describe a rival as "low IQ." If we engage in creepy behavior, we will call other people creepy. If we are insecure, it comes out in "put-downs" of others to make ourselves look good in comparison.

Some psychologists and psychiatrists have suggested that beneath Trump's egotism and narcissism there is a basic insecurity that he has tried to overcome by accumulating wealth and power. Humility is not Trump's strong suit. He is constantly trying to prove to the world (and himself) that he is good enough.

Trump frequently and inappropriately boasts about his incredible wealth and business acumen, his impressively high IQ, his education, being a top student at the best schools, his unmatched golf skills, the fabulous quality of his golf courses, the beauty of his wives, his personal impact on the stock market and employment statistics, calling himself a "stable genius." His magnificent homes, properties, wives, and boastful comments may be intended to mask his insecurities.

The temptation is to paint the other person with the character flaws that he sees in himself but is trying to hide: "lyin'," "little," "slimeball," "nervous," "fatty," "crazy," "creepy," "low IQ," "lightweight," "loser," "dumb as a box of rocks," etc.

Whatever his mental state of mind, it is clear that Trump has little or no respect for other people. He demands absolute personal loyalty from the employees of the US government that work in the executive branch, but Trump has no loyalty to anyone—including his wives.

Unfortunately, Trump is on center stage every day as he models his version of civility and respect to his fellow politicians, his base of voters, and the adults and children of America and the world. He is having a devastating impact on the level of civility and respect in government, business, and traditional American values.

If the American culture ultimately adopts Trump's version of civility and respect, the damage will be felt in every nook and cranny of society. Incivility and disrespect generate divisiveness, anger, violence, rage, and fear. America cannot afford to allow the Trump code of conduct to be the standard for the future.

chapter 10

Fair Play

What if the system's designed
To leave no one intentionally behind?
Offering a fair chance to all
To rise or to fall,
By using or losing one's mind!
JB

A Level Playing Field

There are few concepts that are more widely cherished
in America than fair play. Most of us just want to be allowed
to compete on a level playing field. A privileged few prefer to
have the playing field tilted in their favor and are willing to
pay or cheat for an unfair advantage. In America most people
expect to get a fair shake. Occasionally we are disappointed.

My parents had a total of two years of high school education between them, but they raised their seven children to
believe that every opportunity was available to us. I grew up
expecting that I would be treated fairly no matter what education or career path I chose. I was well aware of the need for
effort and hard work in order to succeed. My parents taught

me that was the American way. I was totally unaware of the concept of privilege.

I played a lot of sports while growing up in a small town in Indiana. Basketball and baseball were my favorites, and both utilized independent judges called umpires in baseball and referees in basketball. It never dawned on me that they might fail to be impartial. I chalked up perceived bad calls to human error.

Sandlot games were played without umpires or referees, and honor was the name of the game. Everyone understood there was no cheating allowed. If there was disagreement on a call, we resolved it and moved on. After all, it was only a game. Playing the game was more important than winning.

Privilege comes in many forms, not all of them involving money. In retrospect I am aware that I was, indeed, privileged. Being a white male, raised in a kind, loving, stable, and encouraging family environment, gave me a huge advantage as I ventured out into the adult world.

Fair Play in Sports

NCAA Division I sport programs are intended to compete on a level playing field. Rules are in place for recruiting and educating student athletes. Many colleges follow the rules. Some schools, coaches, and alumni do not follow the rules, thereby getting an unfair edge over the competition. Sometimes those athletes, coaches, and alumni are caught cheating and banned from future participation—or worse. The ultimate goal is fair play.

Professional sports (and some amateur sports as well) have had to resort to blood tests to minimize cheating by athletes who use illegal enhancement drugs or hormones. Again, the goal is a level playing field for everyone.

Golf is a potential role model for fair play. Almost every experienced golfer is knowledgeable about the rules of golf, and the vast majority of golfers follow the rules religiously. For the most part it is a self-monitoring model. Golfers are expected to call themselves on any rules infractions and accept the required penalties. The game teaches respect for fair play and respect for one another. It is a game based on honor and tradition. There is simply no room for cheating in golf. Golfers who cheat usually find it difficult to find playing partners—unless they own the golf course, as does our current president.

President Trump is the subject of a recent book written by Rick Reilly entitled *Commander in Cheat: How Golf Explains Trump*. In contrast, for most golfers playing fairly and by the rules is a matter of personal pride. It is part of the tradition and allure of the sport. Golf teaches values if we let it.

Fair Play in Business

Having practiced law for decades, one of the lessons I learned early in life was to do what I promised to do. It was a lesson I initially learned from my dad as a young teenager, and relearned in the practice of law. The practice of law is not always easy, but it is also not rocket science. If I told a client that his or her project would be completed within the next ten days, and legal fees would amount to so much, all that I had to do was execute on the promise. The expectation of the client was that I would be competent, fair, timely, and honest. Not only did this practice result in satisfied (and often surprised) clients, but I ended up representing quite a few attorneys in their own legal issues.

Many of my law clients owned small businesses, and I served as their legal counsel. I was impressed with the level of honesty and integrity with which these businesses were managed. Quality product and service were the keys to running a successful business, with profits a by-product of such efforts. These small businesses treated their customers with fairness and respect, thereby avoiding the expenses of litigation and disputes. It was a matter of honor to pay their bills, whether to suppliers, subcontractors, creditors, banks, or professionals. I cannot remember a single incident of being "stiffed" on legal fees by a business client.

The contrast of my business experience with the Trump model is the difference between day and night. If reports are accurate, his businesses were built on disputes, conflicts, litigation, bankruptcies, unpaid subcontractors and suppliers, threats, and stiffing banks and professionals in order to get an unfair advantage in business ("Donald Trump is no role model for business ethics," marketwatch.com). The mission was apparently to make a ton of money, with little or no thought to providing an outstanding product or treating people fairly.

As president, it appears that Trump is running our government much the way he apparently ran his businesses. It is all about money, and incurring trillions in additional debt is irrelevant ("US budget deficit jumps 23.1% over last year as debt crisis looms," CNN). Perhaps he plans to "stiff" our nation's creditors the same way he handled his business debts. Or more likely, he knows that he will be long gone when repayment is due. Future American citizens—our children and grandchildren—will be stuck with the problem.

Fair Play in Politics

Traditionally, campaigning for political office and governing were relatively benign exercises. Most politicians treated each other with respect and tried to represent their constituencies effectively and fairly. They took pride in being "statesmen," and could be relied upon to do the right thing. Voting was limited to legitimate, registered voters, and polling places were safe and impartial. Voter fraud was the exception to the rule. In most parts of the country the democratic system worked very well.

The system has deteriorated in recent years. The opposing party has become the enemy, and cooperation in governing has been severely limited. The system has evolved from largely bipartisan to extremely partisan. Pew Research Center reports that political polarization—the vast and growing gap between liberals and conservatives, Republicans and Democrats—is a defining feature of American politics today. Cooperation for the common good is no longer an option. This disease has spread to federal, state, and local levels. Hypocrisy is driving many qualified people out of politics.

The deterioration began before the Trump administration and has accelerated during his term. It is no longer the goal of politics to serve the people fairly and effectively. Rather, the goal is to win election at any cost. Billions of dollars from largely anonymous sources have flowed into campaigns to influence legislation and governmental policies. Citizens United and other court rulings have obliterated decades of commonsense campaign finance laws. Now a handful of wealthy special interests dominate political funding, often through super PACs and shadowy nonprofits that conceal donors' identities from the public (Brennan Center for Justice). Many politicians are now part of the problem, with no solution in sight.

The Trump election brought to the attention of the world the influence of foreign governments in getting vulnerable politicians elected. Russian efforts to elect Trump are well documented in the Mueller report. It is one thing to have American citizens attempt to influence an election. It is quite another matter to have a hostile foreign government clandestinely influence who will be our elected leaders.

The Russian influence along with misleading polls and falsely planted stories on social media have placed the integrity of the democratic system in doubt. Fair play in politics is missing in action, and it is sorely missed.

The ongoing battle between Trump and Congress is destroying our democratic system based on laws and the Constitution. His obstructionist approach lacks total regard for the powers of Congress. ("Trump's Troubling Rebuke of Congressional Oversight," Brennan Center for Justice). In my opinion, any other president acting as Trump has acted would have been impeached long ago.

Fair Play in Education

Minority groups are very familiar with the tilted field of education. For decades African Americans and Native Americans were limited to segregated and inferior grade schools, high schools, and colleges. It has only been in the past half century that opportunities have been available for everyone to receive a quality education. The playing field is still not level, but the tilt is less pronounced than in prior times. As in business, the ultimate goal is fairness.

Recent allegations of bribery and cheating, which have enabled wealthy parents to buy their children into the best universities, are a step in the wrong direction ("College coaches, celebrities charged in largest-ever admissions bribery case at elite schools," USA Today). In a way, it is a sign of the times. Our role model in the White House is all about money and power. Why would we expect better behavior from wealthy, influential citizens?

Trump's History of Fair Play

Not many young men wanted to be drafted and shipped off to the jungles of Vietnam in the nineteen sixties and early seventies. I admit that I was one of those who did not want to go to war, and between college and law school deferments, marriage, and two children, the draft passed me by. Many others, including such privileged young men as John McCain, Robert Mueller, and John Kerry, did their duty to America and joined the legion of draftees of lesser means to serve their country.

Donald Trump opted to get a letter from his friendly doctor diagnosing bone spurs that would keep him out of the military and active in New York business and social circles. The bone spurs apparently had no detrimental effect on his social life or his fabulous golf game.

Donald Trump and his father, Fred, were sued by the federal government half a century ago for violation of the civil rights laws related to "fair housing." It seems they were refusing to rent apartments in their projects to members of minority groups. Personal interests and greed trumped fair play and the law. He was above the law long before he became president.

Trump was an early and vocal critic of President Obama, demanding to see his birth certificate to prove that Obama was born in the United States and not in Kenya as insinuated by Trump. ("Trump was the most prominent promoter of birther conspiracy theories," wikipedia.org). Trump held on to his "birther" argument for years, alleging that Obama was not the legitimate president. Clearly, Trump knew better but chose to make the ridiculous and unfair allegations to feed raw meat to his bigoted base of supporters. To many of them, it was inconceivable that persons of color deserved to live in the White House—unless they were cooks, butlers, or maids.

As previously indicated, it was apparently standard operating procedure for Trump's businesses to fail to pay their subcontractors, painters, plumbers, and electricians. When confronted, he simply told them to sue him or accept a fraction of what they were owed. Many of these creditors did not have the financial resources or legal teams to fight the mighty Donald and his Roy Cohn-led legal team in court and accepted pennies on the dollar to avoid financial ruin ("Hundreds allege Donald Trump doesn't pay his bills, including dishwashers, waiters, and painters," USA Today). There was nothing fair about the game Trump played with creditors, but it did add to his personal wealth.

During the presidential campaign a number of women alleged sexual affairs with Trump during his most recent marriage. In an apparent violation of campaign finance laws, he reportedly paid hush money to prevent allegations from becoming public and thereby affect his electability ("Everyone involved in the 2016 hush-money payments says they were campaign-related—except Trump," *Washington Post March 11, 2019*) . His actions support the old adage: "All is fair in love and war." Trump's former personal attorney, Michael Cohen, has been disbarred and imprisoned, partly for his participation with Donald Trump in these violations of campaign finance laws. President Trump remains free in the White House.

Consequences of Lack of Fair Play

Words and actions have consequences. Trump's reputation for being unfair in his past business practices and in his campaign for president has shocked most fair-minded Americans. His attitude and activities as president have created chaos. World leaders have become skeptical of his trustworthiness. America's international reputation has taken a nosedive.

chapter 11

Integrity

What if life is a test
Of how close we can be to our best?
A model for living
A life that is giving,
And not about feathering one's nest.

JB

In *Character Building* I described integrity this way:
People of integrity have nothing to hide. They have strong
moral beliefs and tend to live lives based on values, principles,
and a consistency of righteous actions.

The Importance of Integrity

We admire and respect people who exude integrity. There
is an aura of authenticity, stability, inner strength, and calmness that emanates from people with integrity. Such integrity
is particularly important for an American president so that
citizens will know that leadership will have the courage to
be measured, sane, and sensible, no matter the situation.
American values will always prevail.

Our forty-third president, George W. Bush, demonstrated integrity during one of the darkest hours in American history. Immediately following the terrorist attacks of September 11, 2001, President Bush reacted with a calm determination that spread out to an angry and fearful America. He provided the kind of authentic leadership and integrity that was needed at that crucial time in our history.

Integrity is contagious. When a leader demonstrates integrity, it tends to become the standard for followers. Soldiers willingly follow and emulate a military leader like General Eisenhower. A nation followed the integrity of its spiritual leader, Mahatma Gandhi, who taught that "an eye for an eye only ends up making the whole world blind." The courage and integrity of Winston Churchill during the bombing siege of Great Britain spread across the British Empire and around the world.

Trump's Version of Integrity

Growing up in a wealthy, powerful New York family provided a doorway to advantage. Trump was able to get into the most exclusive schools, join influential organizations, live a celebrity lifestyle, have access to great financial resources, and avoid being drafted and sent to Vietnam. The playing field was always tilted in his favor.

As an adult, he could have used his powerful position to be a role model for doing business with integrity. Instead, Trump learned to harness his powerful resources with his natural bullying mentality to beat his competitors into the ground. He was not above misleading and deceiving his business competitors in order to gain an unfair advantage. As previously stated, bullying his creditors allowed him to avoid paying some of his bills and thereby increase his personal wealth.

Grossly exaggerating the value of his assets enabled him to obtain massive bank loans. According to the *Washington Post*, Trump's shaky connection to factual reality also applied to business deals in which he misreported his assets to convince lenders to provide him with funding. Having integrity in business was not a Trump priority.

It was Trump's business reputation that reportedly resulted in being blackballed by NFL owners who prevented him from buying the Buffalo Bills, and by Las Vegas insiders who kept him out of owning casinos in Nevada ("Donald Trump Pulled One Over on America, But He Couldn't Sucker the NFL," the daily beast.com).

The shady business practices took on an even more sinister look with the power of the presidency. Personal enrichment and enhancement of power have taken priority over doing the right thing. Smoke and mirrors have replaced transparency in government. The trust in government by the average American has rarely been lower.

How Do We Bring Integrity Back into American Government?

It is vitally important to the future of America that we have a government with integrity and openness. It is becoming increasingly clear that will not happen during the Trump era. America needs to move forward in a new direction. That direction needs to responsibly deal with the immense challenges facing our nation and the world. Government leaders who have been playing political games need to be replaced by leaders with integrity who are ready to focus on solutions to such pressing problems as:

➢ joining the rest of planet Earth in addressing global warming and climate change;

➢ working together with allies to reduce dangers posed by potentially violent regimes;

➢ finding a way for all Americans to have access to affordable health care;

➢ facing and resolving the opioid crisis in America;

➢ passing common sense gun control legislation;

➢ enacting comprehensive, fair, and sensible immigration reform;

➢ rebuilding the crumbling infrastructure in America;

➢ developing legislation that supports and expands the middle class and narrows the gap between the haves and have-nots; and

➢ creating a kinder, less fearful environment that promotes justice and opportunity for all.

Helping One Another

What if we're in this together,
In sunny or stormy weather?
What if survival requires
We have generous desires
And freely help one another?
JB

The Case for Giving.

There have been adages about giving that have been around since before Jesus walked the earth. It has been said that giving and receiving are the same. Karma indicates that what goes around comes around. We tend to get back what we give out. The more we give, the more we receive. The kinder and more generous we are, the better we are treated in return. This basic concept has been a foundation of Christianity and most other religions as well. It is also good business and good government to help one another.

The happiest people I know are the ones who are focused on giving. Their mission is to be truly helpful to everyone, everywhere. In the words of Kahlil Gibran:

And there are those who give and know not
pain in their giving, nor do they seek joy, nor
give mindfulness of virtue; they give as in yon-
der valley the myrtle breathes its fragrance
into space, through the hands of such as these
God speaks, and from behind their eyes He
smiles upon the Earth.

Conversely, the saddest, angriest people I know are the
ones who are focused on taking. There is not enough stuff in
the world to fully satisfy a person focused on taking. A taker
simply cannot get enough money, homes, properties, power,
wives, sex partners, food, alcohol, drugs, toys, etc. Prisons are
filled with people focused on taking.

America has a rich history and tradition of giving. Perhaps
the greatest example of this American value was the Marshall
Plan, a.k.a. the European Recovery Program. The United
States voluntarily initiated aid to Western Europe following the devastation of World War II. Named after Secretary
of State General George C. Marshall, the plan gave billions
of dollars in economic assistance to help rebuild Western
Europe's economies. An additional goal was to halt the spread
of communism in Europe (History Channel). Our gifts and
example were instrumental in establishing democratic forms
of government in many European nations after World War
II. The friendships and trade relations that resulted have benefited the United States as well and have led to formation of
NATO, a strategic alliance to protect Western Europe (and
America) from a hawkish Soviet Union.

The United States is heavily populated with churches and
charitable organizations whose mission is to help those in
need. Nongovernmental organizations (NGOs) such as the
International Rescue Committee, Mercy Corps, and PATH

are headquartered in the United States and provide services worldwide, with emphasis on needs in Third World countries. Successful businesspeople such as Bill and Melinda Gates, Robert F. Smith, and Warren Buffet have placed much of their wealth into charitable foundations to be given away for unselfish, charitable purposes. Ordinary people make it a point to take care of neighbors and sometimes total strangers. America is a nation of givers, and that is a good thing.

On This Journey Together

Planet Earth has been divided up in countless ways. We are divided into continents, regions, nations, forms of government, religious beliefs, political persuasions, ethnic cultures, languages, climates, skin colors, levels of wealth or poverty, education levels, genders, age groups, warriors and pacifists, rurals and urbanites, givers and takers. It is understandable how we tend to bunch together and isolate ourselves from the "others" as if they were aliens from another planet.

Beneath our differences, however, the human essence is remarkably the same. We are more alike than it may appear on the surface, and we are in this human experience together. A dust storm in Africa may affect weather conditions in North America or Europe; a melting glacier in the Arctic may cause deadly flooding in Southeast Asia; a religious culture of radical terrorism may wreak havoc on innocent victims a continent away; an attitude that white-skinned people are somehow superior to dark-skinned people can result in centuries of slavery and discrimination; weaponry developed in "advanced" civilizations can wipe out "others" in a flash. It is time to recognize that we are all interdependent on each other if planet Earth and human civilization is to survive into the twenty-second century.

The Trumpian Record

The experience of the now-defunct Trump Foundation should have been a warning of President Trump's approach to giving. From 2009 on, this "charity" was funded exclusively with other people's money. Trump, on the other hand, used the foundation's resources for his personal purposes. In 2016 Trump admitted to the Internal Revenue Service that the foundation violated a legal prohibition against "self dealing." Rather than benefiting charitable causes, Trump was using the foundation for his own personal and political benefit. The Trump Foundation was subsequently dissolved in disgrace ("Trump Foundation Will Dissolve, Accused of Shocking Pattern of Illegality," *New York Times December 18, 2018*).

President Trump has been extremely generous with his superrich supporters, pushing for major reductions in taxes for corporations and America's richest individuals. They, in turn, have filled his political coffers with generous "investments" in future tax policies and lax business regulations. He has been less generous to the needy, cutting funds in such places as social safety nets for the poor, regulatory agencies intended to protect consumers from predatory practices, public education, access to health care, and aid to "s—t hole" countries.

It is no wonder that our president always appears to be so angry, bitter, attacking, and sad.

Immigrants have felt the wrath of Trump's less than helpful attitude. Asylum seekers from Central America have been turned away and sometimes separated from their children in the process ("Migrant children are being separated from parents," *Texas Tribune July 13, 2019*). Undocumented people who have been living and working in America for years, raising their families and paying taxes, have been deported back to countries they have not lived in for decades. ("ICE begins nationwide raids on undocumented immigrants," Reason.com).

Affordable health care has been eroded from millions of low- and middle-income Americans. Trump's personal priority has been to erase President Obama's health-care legacy rather than giving a helping hand to millions of Americans in desperate need of health care.

Foreign aid has been reduced or eliminated for poorer nations, including the Central American countries that have been the source of asylum seekers to America. Ironically, reducing such foreign aid just worsens the drastic conditions in Central America, resulting in even more asylum seekers at our southern border ("Trump plans to cut aid to El Salvador, Honduras and Guatemala over migrant fight," *Washington Post March 30, 2019*).

As with just about every policy in the Trump administration, giving is all about the money. If there is nothing in the giving to directly benefit the giver, the conditional gift is quickly eliminated. Giving is "the art of the deal" in Trump's mind. He only gives to get something in return.

Restoring a Helping Attitude

America has been incredibly blessed. It is one of the richest countries in the world. It got there partially due to its generous and helping attitude. America is a nation full of givers who are happily helping their fellow citizens and others to succeed in life. America deserves a leader who is in sync with the generosity of many of its citizens.

Chapter 13

Tolerance/Diversity

What if we all were the same
In looks, behavior, and name?
If we thought the same way
And received the same pay,
It would be such a boring game!
JB

Meaning of Tolerance

It is not always easy to recognize, respect, and appreciate an opinion or behavior that is different than our own. There is a natural human tendency to think that my perspective is the correct one. Tolerance does not necessarily require that we agree and/or share such differences, but it does require an openness to consider and appreciate different viewpoints.

Being broad-minded is a consciousness that can take effort and exercise. A willingness to see a larger picture than the obvious is a common characteristic of successful entrepreneurs. One of the keys to the success of so many American business organizations is a cultural appreciation for new approaches to solving problems. Innovation and creativity are valued and welcomed by many successful businesses. The most valuable American worker is not a robot.

American voters have embraced diversity in the election to Congress of a number of women of color. They bring a new and fresh perspective to "making America great." Trump's response has been to urge them to go back to where they came from if they don't like his policies for America. Chants from the Trump cult at his campaign rallies ring of "send her back," a racist chant that has no place in America.

Historically, dictatorships and theocracies have demonstrated a lack of tolerance as a form of social and mind control. Anyone with a tendency to resist (i.e., free thinker, maverick, rebel) was cruelly suppressed or eliminated. Only the docile remained standing in line.

The absence of tolerance often leads to hate, abuse, isolationism, radicalism, and even terrorism. The world has witnessed the devastating effects of intolerance in Nazi Germany, Eastern European countries during the Cold War, Russia, China, North Korea, and a number of Middle East theocracies.

Diversity in America

Diversity is a challenge for tolerance. Appreciation of diversity is not an automatic human instinct. America is blessed with diversity of race, ethnicity, languages, economic status, age, gender, education, and religion, to name a few. Discrimination is an ever-present danger among diverse groups.

Race, ethnicity, sexual orientation, and religion are probably the most frequent subjects of discrimination in America. Discrimination can have an impact on life experiences, including: where we are free to live, our educational opportunities, likely careers and level of earnings, circle of friends, self-esteem, and even the odds and length of incarceration.

And yet diversity is one of the most cherished traits in America. Deep down, there is an understanding that differences of opinion and perspectives are what make us strong. Diversity is an asset.

The American Ideal

Inscribed on the Statue of Liberty is this welcoming message to immigrants: "Give me your tired, your poor, your huddled masses yearning to breathe free, the wretched refuse of your teeming shores. Send these, the homeless tempest-tossed to me, I lift my lamp beside the golden door" (Emma Lazarus).

To say that immigration values have changed in the Trump era would be a gross understatement, as asylum seekers are routinely detained in cages, and families are separated by the Trump administration. Undocumented residents, some of whom have lived in America for decades, are rounded up and deported. The open and welcoming America is no more—at least for now.

Beneath all of our superficial differences, we are all spiritual beings engaged on a common human journey. We are fellow travelers on planet Earth, and we can help each other and learn from each other if we are willing to overlook differences. It all depends on our focus. We see what we value and want to see.

Ideally in America, as the melting pot continues its work of bringing us closer together, the culture will evolve, and our focus will shift further away from our differences and closer to our common goals.

Trumpian Attitudes

Diversity appears to be a threat to Trump. Clearly, his preference is to surround himself in government with wealthy white men—people who think like him, but obviously not as well as the self-declared stable genius ("Trump's Cabinet is more white and more male than any first Cabinet since Ronald Reagan's," Center for American Progress).

Walls and the costs of membership keep the riffraff out of his golf resorts. His Trump Tower residence looks down upon the masses far below. His privileged background, private schooling, and wealth have provided a buffer between Trump and the American people. This background makes it all the more astounding that he has built a cult-like following among the poorly educated and underprivileged segments of American society. It only makes sense if race is the defining issue.

The Mexican border wall is an attempt to prevent the riffraff from entering the United States, and it has little to do with terrorism or drugs. (There is no proposed wall on our northern border, because most Canadians look a lot like us.) The ban on Muslims entering our country is a blatant attempt to preserve the status quo of a "white Christian nation." His comfort zone does not appear to include tolerance or diversity.

Chapter 14

Family/Community

What if we all felt connected,
A sense of belonging detected?
Working and playing as one
Toward a goal like just having fun?
Might we feel a lot less rejected?

JB

What Do Family Values Mean in America?

Family means more than a group of related people. It also connotes a feeling of love, safety, security, and sense of belonging. Ideally, family is a group of people we can trust and rely on when help is needed. Family is the basic unit, the building block for our support, protection, and development.

Family also provides a classroom for learning and understanding such basic concepts as love, morals, trust, teamwork, discipline, responsibility, values, and ideals. Growing up in a healthy, functional family is worth more than a multimillion-dollar inheritance. It develops a mind-set, a foundation, and a framework for a successful life.

Dysfunctional families can present obstacles to the growth and development of family members. Dysfunction can be the result of poverty, ignorance, quality of education, level of common sense, health issues, mental illness, emotional instability, addictions, premature deaths, and selfish, irresponsible attitudes. Many dysfunctional families pass their patterns on from generation to generation. It is a rare and courageous person who can break free of such a family environment and become a successful, highly functioning individual.

So, family values in America can mean different things to different people. Ideally, however, the concept is that the family works as a team—the fundamental unit of American society upon which its values are derived.

Community

Beyond the family is the concept of community. It is a group of people who share common interests, goals, and attitudes. America is made up of many different types of communities. Communities may or may not have a shared physical location.

Most people want a sense of connection with others. Connectivity can be found in such organizations and places as churches, schools, political organizations, labor unions, fraternities and sororities, alumni groups, neighborhood pubs, country clubs, gangs, fraternal organizations, athletic teams, book clubs, support groups, professional associations, workplaces, internet chat rooms, etc. Communities are the lifeblood of America.

Communities tend to have structure, leadership, philosophies, and common goals. Their impact on the lives of Americans can be positive or negative. For example, being a volunteer worker for Habitat for Humanity may promote life-skills, responsibility, kindness, and caring for others. Conversely, being a member of the Ku Klux Klan or a neo-Nazi group may instill attitudes of hatred, bigotry, and violence. A member of a criminal gang or the Mob may be instilled with violent, destructive values.

Family and community are double-edged swords, depending on their values and shared goals. Leadership is a key element in establishing the direction of the group. Sometimes a community may have positive members and goals (e.g., the Catholic Church), but leadership sometimes misdirects the church in an incredibly negative way (e.g., fostering a breeding ground for pedophile priests aided and abetted by top church officials who cover up the crimes).

The US Senate and the House of Representatives are both communities with shared goals. They have the potential to represent the American citizens by governing responsibly, enacting laws that are in the best interests of the people. In fact, that is their job description. Sometimes, however, congressional leadership forgets its priorities and makes choices that are detrimental to the common good. Power and greed sometimes overpower common sense. American values can be lost in the hypocrisy.

The Trump Administration

In a sense, the Trump administration is both a family and a community. Both Trump's daughter, Ivanka, and his son-in-law, Jared Kushner, play major advisory roles in his administration. Kushner has reportedly used his position to arrange loans for his family's business interests, with some of the money coming from the Middle East, where he is supposedly brokering peace ("Having Jared Kushner and his wife,

Ivanka, Trump's daughter, working in the White House is a case study of nepotism gone nuts," *Guardian March 6, 2018*).

The community consists of a cast of characters revolving in and out of the doors of government. As of the summer of his third year in office, fourteen members of the Trump cabinet have resigned or been fired. Sixty-six percent of all senior-level staffers who came into their jobs along with Trump are now gone (CNN Politics). This community's shared goal is supposed to be to govern a complex federal bureaucracy and serve the needs of the American people. According to the Mueller report, the shared goal seems to have evolved into protecting the president from criminal indictment and/or impeachment. Chaos reigns in the Trump administration, and the community has become dysfunctional.

chapter 15

Confidence

What if leadership trust is unfounded
Based on blustery boasts that sounded
Like he knew what to do
But in truth had no clue?
It would leave the voters astounded!
JB

Can-Do Attitude

America has been built on a foundation of the self-confidence and can-do attitude of its leaders and citizens. As a people, we have a rich tradition of believing in ourselves. Our record over the past two plus centuries demonstrates that this confidence is well-founded. Self-confidence has been a key to success. We have earned the respect and envy of much of the world. Confidence is an important American value.

Building confidence is a process that involves facing our fears, acting with integrity, preparation, wisdom, strength, courage, and learning from mistakes and losses. No one who is alive and active goes through life without making mistakes. It is the very nature of being human. The wise person learns from past mistakes and makes smarter choices in the future.

As a nation, America has experienced its share of mistakes and has usually rebounded stronger and wiser for them. This long track record is exactly what drives my confidence and trust that America can rebound from the Trump era, stronger and wiser than ever.

True Confidence

Elizabeth Kubler-Ross described confidence thus: "People are like stained-glass windows. They sparkle and shine when the sun is out, but when the darkness sets in their true beauty is revealed only if there is light from within." Real confidence cannot be faked because it is an inner strength that goes way beyond empty boasting. An astute observer can discern if there is a light on inside.

People in leadership roles do not always have all the answers. Real leaders, however, are willing to listen to advice, consider options and alternatives, and trust that the problem can be solved. They believe in themselves and are open to fresh ideas. Being intimidating and defensive does not connote confidence and is not a strong leadership quality; being open, non-defensive, and self-assured is the strong way to lead.

According to Dr. Stephen Covey, author of *Principle Centered Leadership*, truly confident leaders "live in harmony with fairness, equity, justice, integrity, honesty and trust. They are not into using their power to control other people or gain sexual favors. Their focus is on being of service." This is the way to ignite that inner light described by Elizabeth Kubler-Ross. Any other way is a con game or ruse.

False Confidence

We have all experienced situations in which we were asked to perform beyond our own perceived capabilities. It's an uncomfortable feeling. We put on a confident front, prepare as best we can, and work to the best of our ability for the best result. It's kind of a "fake it until you make it" mentality, learning to overcome fears and self-doubts. Sometimes that works out, and we learn and grow from the experience. I don't see that as false confidence. It is part of stretching our limits, living a productive, effective life. Come to think of it, that was the way that I learned to practice law. It's probably the reason they call it a "practice."

By false confidence I mean the blustery, boastful, intimidation tactics that some people use to bully their way to a result. They pretend to know, but in reality don't have a clue—and they're not open to learning the facts or considering alternatives. False confidence is a process that has no place in the leadership of government, business, or anything else that affects other people.

Confidence in Government

Despite Ronald Reagan's famous quote about the most terrifying words in English: "I'm from the government and I'm here to help," trust in the federal government has been as high as 80 percent at times in our history. Trust in government began eroding in the sixties amid the Vietnam War and in the seventies following Watergate. In the Trump era, public trust is at an all-time low (Pew Research Center).

In my experience, the best way to build trust in a government or another person is by having them lead by good example. Being consistent, reliable, keeping promises, telling the truth, and being brutally honest and transparent go a long way toward creating trust and confidence. The quickest way to lose trust is to be erratic, dishonest, deceitful, and treat people with disrespect. The latter is a portrait of President Trump.

chapter 16

Education/Knowledge

What if it was common knowledge
That everyone could afford college?
Would it narrow the gap
And provide a road map
For eluding the poverty trap?
JB

The Value of Education

Education is a process for acquiring knowledge, helping us
to understand life. Knowledge is a key to enriching our lives.
According to Nelson Mandela: "Education is the most powerful weapon you can use to change the world." It has been
an American tradition to promote education for everyone,
not just for the elite.

My family of origin was somewhat typical of families in
rural America in the early part of the twentieth century. My
parents were both born in the late eighteen nineties and were
of school age in the years before World War I. In rural areas
of Indiana, a high school was not always locally available.

Dad took advantage of a nearby Benedictine Monastery to acquire two years of high school before his dad died, and he returned home to run the family farm. Mom had no options for continuing school after the eighth grade and went to work as a domestic maid in Louisville.

Fortunately, education opportunities have changed dramatically since that early twentieth century era. By the middle of the century, high schools and colleges were readily available to me and my siblings. Both of our parents encouraged their children to go to college following high school graduation. Five of the seven children availed ourselves of the college opportunity, paying our own way through college with scholarships, supplemented by loans (my older brother Joe was a CPA and my "banker"), and summer and part-time jobs after school. To us, it was very important to take advantage of an opportunity not available to our parents.

A highly developed system of educational institutions has evolved throughout the United States. State-sponsored universities and schools of higher education now populate every state in the union. In addition, private schools abound, sponsored by churches or private individuals and organizations.

Liberal vs. Technical

Some traditional universities have a tendency to focus on liberal arts and business degrees, with areas of studies covering such subjects as history, government, math, science, journalism, sociology, psychology, languages, geology, anthropology, music, accounting, finance, engineering, agriculture, and the like. In my home state of Indiana, these schools include Indiana University, Purdue University, Ball State University, Indiana State University, University of Southern Indiana, and a myriad of private schools such as the University of Notre

Dame and Butler University. Their goal is to graduate students who are well-rounded in their educations.

These universities also offer graduate-level programs in specific studies, such as medicine, dentistry, teaching, mental health, science, business, and the law.

Some schools of higher education focus on computer sciences, nursing, specialty trades, and technical areas that teach practical job skills. My niece, Sue Elsperman, is president of Indiana Vocational and Technical College (IVY Tech) which has nineteen campuses spread around the state of Indiana and more than one hundred thousand students. IVY Tech offers a practical, less "ivory tower" approach to higher education.

Neither approach to education is better or worse than the other. It is a matter of a student finding an area of study that best meets the student's needs and interests. The American education system is intended to provide an opportunity for anyone motivated to follow his or her American dream.

The Pursuit of Knowledge

Knowledge, in and of itself, is a worthwhile endeavor. It is the goal of most universities. Knowledge can also be acquired outside the educational system, in such places as the family, workplace, church, the military, self-study, and nature. The education system does not have a monopoly on learning, but it is a helpful vehicle for many people.

The value of knowledge cannot be overestimated. The world is powered by knowledge, and it is essential for anyone wanting to be involved and engaged in worldly activities. Without the active pursuit of knowledge, life would be boring and unrewarding.

Trump's Approach to Education

Having attended exclusive schools all his young life, it might be expected that our president would be a strong promoter of education for all Americans. He frequently boasts about his outstanding education and scholastic record. He attended a private boarding school, then Fordham University and the Wharton School of Business. He likes to talk about his educational accomplishments: "I went to the Wharton School of Business. I'm, like, a really smart person." Passing those advantages on to future generations would be a natural expectation from such a wonderfully privileged student.

A pro-education administration would logically promote:

➢ widening the reach and quality of early-childhood educational opportunities,

➢ beefing up the budgets of the public elementary and high school programs,

➢ taking steps to enhance school safety issues that protect students and teachers from the rampant gun violence that has devastated so many schools and students,

➢ encouraging after-school programs that give students in poor school districts an edge in learning while simultaneously protecting them from gang violence and drugs in their neighborhoods,

➢ valuing and appreciating teachers in the public school system, and

➢ establishing standards that ensure that students have every opportunity to succeed.

Instead, Trump's first step as the "education president" was to appoint a secretary of education who has a long history of promoting private, for-profit schools at the expense of the public school system. Betsy DeVos is known for her support for school choice, voucher programs, and charter schools (Wikipedia).

The billionaire secretary has diverted moneys otherwise available for public education, focusing instead on for-profit charter and church-sponsored schools catering to the "higher classes." Trump's personal focus quickly shifted to cutting taxes for the rich and reducing educational and other benefits to the rest of America.

A priority of many Americans is to make higher education more affordable. The administration has done nothing to relieve the student debt load of those Americans who have followed their dream to get an education in order to build a better life. Neither has it done anything to make education more affordable for current and prospective students. For many Americans, higher education is out of financial reach during the Trump era.

Years before his presidential run, Trump was involved in creating Trump University, a for-profit company that ran a real estate training program from 2005 to 2010. When the "school" was established, the New York State Education Department warned that it was in violation of New York's educational licensing laws (*National Review*). Trump ignored the warning and proceeded to enroll students in his school. Multiple individual lawsuits and class action lawsuits ensued from the enrollees, depicting Trump University as a bait and switch scam costing "students" as much as $35,000. In 2016 a federal court approved a $25 million settlement with students who claimed they were duped by Trump University. The "university" is now defunct but continues to serve as an indicator of Trump's approach to education. Yes, Trump University was a massive scam (*National Review*).

The Consequences

There is a direct correlation between education and prosperity. The highly educated tend to earn higher incomes than their less educated fellow Americans. By dampening the educational opportunities of the poor and focusing on educating the better off, Trump has continued in his efforts to widen the divide between rich and poor in America. At least he has been consistent in his approach, with education policies following the example of his economic policies.

chapter 17

Questioning

What if we believed and were sold,
Every official proclamation we're told?
If we just went along,
Though authority seemed wrong,
Afraid to be left out in the cold?
JB

Freedom to Question Authority

It is a proud and valued American tradition to be bold and unafraid to ask questions. Critical thinking is a characteristic that underlies the American experience. Governmental authorities can be freely doubted and questioned without damaging repercussions. This is one of the biggest differences between the American democratic experience and the experience in nations ruled by autocratic dictators.

I could not be writing this book in Iran, Saudi Arabia, North Korea, China, or Russia. My right to be critical of government officials and policies would be squelched. I would likely disappear, possibly in small pieces, as a result of my stated opinions. It is the difference between living in an open, free, and democratic society versus an authoritarian society. It worries me that President Trump most admires and respects the authoritarian leaders of the world. He acts like he wants to take America in that direction.

Being Open, Truthful, and Non-defensive to Questions Asked

Many members of the free press are dedicated to asking the hard questions, digging deep down to the true essence of the situation. They are effective investigators and interrogators, searching for the truth and exposing deceptions. Most American presidents have not necessarily enjoyed the tough questions but have answered them to the best of their ability. A few presidents have failed the test.

President Trump (along with his spokespersons) has a track record of blocking, obscuring, deceiving, misleading, blaming, intimidating, and outright lying. "Alternative facts" that pop into his head out of nowhere appear to take precedence over reality. *The Urban Dictionary* defines alternative facts as bald-faced lies usually told by someone who is either delusional or a psychopathic liar.

Freedom of information has been substantially curtailed. Trump, his press secretaries, and his advisers employ alternative facts to obstruct and deceive the American public.

Disrespecting the Questioners

In the Trump administration, there is a recognizable pattern for dealing with difficult questions or critical comments. When logical thinking cannot rationalize a behavior or policy, the fallback position is to attack the questioner. Tweets fill cyberspace with accusations such as "fake news," "enemies of the people," "failing *New York Times*," on and on literally hundreds of times like a broken record.

In the case of the Robert Mueller investigation into Russian interference in the 2016 election, the Trump campaign's possible involvement in the interference, and Trump's subsequent efforts to obstruct justice, there was no acknowledgement of the interference or suggestions of policies to avoid the problem in future US elections. Instead, a daily defensive barrage of total denial of Russian influence was launched, describing the investigation as a "hoax," a "witch hunt" conducted by "eighteen angry Democrats." Recently, the Trump approach has evolved into an investigation of the investigators by the beleaguered Justice Department. At Trump's request, Attorney General William Barr is investigating the Russian investigation (NPR).

The Trump strategy has infected much of the executive branch of government. His spokespersons have adopted a similar attitude of derision and intimidation toward the press; members of the cabinet have mimicked the behavior of the president (before passing through the revolving door after a few months in government); some members of Congress have exhibited a toady approach as if the president was an all-powerful and all-knowing deity whose behavior was acceptable for a god.

Consequences

Squelching freedom of thought and its expression are commonplace in authoritarian regimes. It is how they hold on to power. History is populated by despots who held the people in check in order to accomplish their goals. It was the Nazi Germany way; it is the Russian and Chinese way; it is the Middle Eastern way; it is the North Korean way; it is not the American way.

I strongly believe that the American people and the democratic form of government deserve and expect better than we have observed in the Trump White House. Critical thinking and questioning of authority are too strongly embedded in the American culture to allow this approach to continue—whether under a continued Trump presidency or under his successors.

chapter 18

Peace Loving

What if our safety lies
In non-defensive replies?
What if the decision to fight
Is not always right?
JB

A Way of Living

The American people have a long history of preferring peace over conflict. There are always exceptions, but most of us do not go out of our way to look for a fight. We are, by and large, a peace-loving culture. Our churches and our institutions teach peace over war and inner peace over turmoil and anger. We are mostly a friendly, helpful, gentle lot. Our daily battles are fought symbolically on football fields, basketball courts, and in sports arenas.

During the twentieth century it was a reluctant America that was pulled into the European and Asian wars that threatened world peace. Our limited role in those world wars was to restore the peace and stability of civilization. When we have forgotten this role and have acted warlike, it has not worked out so great in places such as Vietnam, Iraq, and Afghanistan.

Sometimes it is necessary to fight when there is abusive behavior, violence, criminal activities, or terrorism. In America, those fights are handled primarily by law enforcement officials and the judicial system. Vigilante justice is generally not appreciated in twenty-first century America.

Law-Abiding

America is a nation of laws. The vast majority of Americans make an honest effort to comply with the laws of the land, perhaps because those laws were enacted by elected officials who represent the wishes of the people. Laws reflect the values of society. Judges interpret the laws and apply them consistently, based on established precedent. The goal in America is for everyone to be treated in a fair and just manner. No one is above the law—not even the president. Our second president, John Adams, said it best: "We are a nation of laws, not of men."

Nonviolent

America has developed a legal system and societal framework that encourages people to live their lives free from fear. The root of all attack is fear. Freedom from fear is essential to experiencing inner peace. Societal peace begins with inner peace among individuals within the citizenry.

The goal of peace-loving people is to resolve conflict and disagreements in a civil, nonthreatening, nonviolent manner. Most sane Americans would not even consider taking justice into their own hands—resorting to violent responses to perceived hurts. Violent behavior is discouraged, and vigilante justice is not acceptable. A legal system is in place, intended for the handling of disputes.

Dealing with Conflict

The practice of law provided me with insights into dealing with conflict. As a young attorney I was frequently in the middle of family battles. Divorces and child custody situations are fertile grounds for anger and conflict. After years of experience on the battlefield, I chose to become a certified family mediator. It was a kinder, gentler alternative for resolving conflict at the end of a marriage or relationship.

As a family mediator, I learned that most divorcing couples were open to an alternative to fighting. They hungered for a way to peacefully and fairly resolve their legal and personal issues and cooperate together in the raising of their children. It did not have to be an expensive legal battle with winners and losers.

My experience indicates there are multiple choices for reacting to conflict. When confronted, we can choose to be:

- ➢ Afraid
- ➢ Angry
- ➢ Defensive
- ➢ Blaming
- ➢ Denying
- ➢ Bullying
- ➢ Acknowledging
- ➢ Non-defensive
- ➢ Solution oriented
- ➢ Apologetic
- ➢ Sincere, genuine, and unafraid

The Trump Approach

As I observe President Trump's reactions to criticism or confrontation, I see only fear and anger. Fearful anger seems to be the essence of his being. His is a system of defensiveness, blaming, attacking, denying, bullying, and rage. From my perspective, it is a very low level of functioning that leads to name-calling, belittling, insulting, and threatening people who do not agree with him. It certainly does not lead to peaceful solutions. Rather, it fuels the battle. ("Trump's defensiveness and denial puts America at risk," *Bangor Daily News October 3, 2017*).

America deserves a leader who is in sync with the peaceful nature of its people. The longer Trump leads our nation, the more his style of anger infects the citizenry, and the greater is the divide among the people.

Independent/
Interdependent

What if we depend on each other
And willingly help one another?
Wouldn't life be a groan
If we lived it alone,
Versus sharing it with a brother?

JB

Democratic Self-Governance

Many Americans have traditionally tended to be independent-minded. Most of us don't like to be told how to act, what to think, where to live, or with whom to share our lives. We prefer to form our own opinions and beliefs. Big government can be an intrusion into our lives. Laws and regulations can feel limiting.

On July 4, 1776, the Declaration of Independence announced to the world America's rejection of British rule. It was drafted primarily by Thomas Jefferson and was courageously signed by fifty-six delegates to the Second Continental Congress.

Early American colonists sacrificed everything to throw off the yoke of foreign rule. The Revolutionary War was fought to gain that proclaimed independence from England and King George. Foreign rule was replaced with a democratic system of self-governance that remains a model to the world nearly two and a half centuries later.

Interconnected with Each Other

Notwithstanding that independent, self-sufficient attitude, those same colonists banded together and helped each other in the fight for independence. They were interdependent, even as they fought for independence. They stayed connected in the formation of the new system of governance that bound thirteen former colonies into the United States of America.

Interconnectivity has been an American value since the very beginning. The Civil War was fought to prevent the secession of slave states from free states, which would have destroyed the Union. The value and importance of interdependence and interconnectivity has only grown as America has developed and become a member of the global community.

Interconnected with the World

In the twenty-first century, America is part of a global community. Business interests are international in scope. Markets for our goods and services are not confined to the United States of America. Manufacturing facilities in Asia, South America, Mexico, Canada, and Europe market their products in America. American companies and farmers sell their products all over the world. Multinational companies dominate the world markets. Commerce does not see borders; it sees opportunities.

In addition to the world of business, continents and nations are interdependent on each other for maintaining world peace, dealing with global climate issues, containing the spread of contagious diseases, and fighting international terrorism.

The Great Wall of China may have protected the Chinese Empire in centuries past. Border walls are no longer an effective model in the twenty-first century.

Trump's Values

Trump is all about trade wars, tariffs, and border walls to separate the United States from its global neighbors. He is trying to take us back in time. It is a separation philosophy in an interconnected world, and it is out of sync with the times.

Trump's philosophy of separation also applies within the United States. The divide between the haves and the have-nots continues to grow under Trump's rule. It grows as a result of his tax policies, education opportunities, racist rhetoric, immigration policies, voter suppression efforts, political appointments, attacks on anyone who disagrees with him, and religious bias.

The right to vote is an important American value that has been won over a long period of time. Women did not get the right to vote until a century ago. Having lost the Civil War and the right to own slaves, southern states passed Jim Crow laws to deny voting rights to the poor and racial minorities. The Voting Rights Act of 1965 was intended to put an end to voter suppression tactics, giving all adult American citizens this basic American right. Unfortunately, during the Trump era voter suppression tactics have resurfaced and multiplied in America ("Voter-Suppression Tactics in the Age of Trump," *New Yorker October 29, 2018*).

According to the Mueller report, the Trump campaign welcomed and accepted the help of Russia to influence the 2016 presidential election in favor of Trump and against his opponent, Hillary Clinton. Rather than being alarmed by such hostile interference in the American democratic system, Trump's response was total denial. As a result, America remains vulnerable to Russian interference in future elections as well. Our hard-fought independence is in jeopardy.

chapter 20

Loving Kindness

What if the Golden Rule
Was considered the crown jewel
Of American values?
"Do unto others
As you would have them do unto you."
JB

The Golden Rule

I believe that most Americans live in accordance with this biblical advice of treating other people the way we would want to be treated. Although its origin may be in religion, its basic message extends to business, politics, family, community, and everyday living. It is a basic principle that leads to successful businesses and to successful lives.

As a traditional value, the Golden Rule has been instrumental in making America a great nation. It is responsible for the social safety nets such as Social Security, Medicare, Medicaid, welfare, and the many churches and charitable organizations that help to care for those in need—in America and around the world.

America is blessed with a vast army of volunteers and donors ready to pitch in when disaster strikes. Neighbors help neighbors to survive hurricanes, tornadoes, floods, wildfires, and earthquakes. Acts of kindness are not limited to disasters in America. Charitable foundations help students with grants and scholarships to attend college; food banks and soup kitchens feed the hungry and the homeless; mentoring programs pass on knowledge from old-timers to younger generations; retirees assist hospitals, libraries, schools, churches, and many other social organizations in providing services to those in need.

These are the people who truly make America great!

The Trumpian Golden Rule

Empathy for other people is not part of President Trump's mental or emotional makeup. His version of loving kindness is to give in order to get something in return. It is all about the art of the deal. The goal is always to take more than what is given. If personal power or enrichment is not forthcoming, there is no "give" in Trump. To paraphrase President John F. Kennedy, Trump's mentality appears to be: "Ask not what you can do for others. Ask what others can do for you." It is the Golden Rule turned upside down.

Consequences of an Absence of Loving Kindness

America has witnessed the effects of Trump's Golden Rule in plain sight:

> ➢ When journalists ask him questions that may not be flattering to him, he turns on them with rude, abusive behavior. "You are a rude, terrible person." Trump attacked CNN reporter Jim Acosta for challenging him

on the alleged "migrant caravan" that was headed for our southern border (*New York Times*). Rather than dealing with questions he does not like, he attacks, belittles, and blackballs the questioner.

➢ When an official of the Justice Department, or an FBI agent, or a member of his legal team, refuses to honor his illegal requests, his reaction is to blame them for his legal problems, attack them, and then fire them.

➢ When a federal judge issues a ruling that is not in his favor, the judge is described as "crooked" or "biased."

➢ When his former personal attorney, Michael Cohen, tells the truth under oath during the Mueller investigation, he is described as a "liar" and "loser."

➢ As a businessman, it was Trump's policy to attempt to weasel out of paying for work done by others on his behalf.

We have yet to witness Trump's reaction if Republican senators and members of Congress someday fail to appease him. Perhaps fear of his bullying reaction is the reason so many legislators have stayed in line for so long. Heaven help them if members of Trump's "base" ever decide to question his policies or behaviors. An impeachment proceeding will place a lot of legislators under pressure to make clear to the world their attitude toward their president. It could prove interesting and enlightening.

chapter 21

Blessed/Grateful

What if an increased awareness
Of justice and fairness
Lighted our hearts and our minds?
Would we thank the Divine
For this democratic design
Of government for all of mankind?
JB

Gratitude for the Founding Fathers

America's Founding Fathers were ahead of their times in the latter part of the eighteenth century. America was founded on the concept that all citizens were free to pursue life, liberty, and happiness. It was a lofty goal that has not always been met for all people in the nearly two and one half centuries since our nation's founding. Notwithstanding its inconsistent application, the US Constitution, along with its first ten amendments (the Bill of Rights) and subsequent constitutional amendments established a blueprint for a level of freedom never before experienced by any civilized nation in recorded history.

The Constitution was a negotiated compromise, with a blend of needs and concerns from every corner of colonial America. The end result was a three-legged stool of coequal branches of government, with Article I being the legislative, Article II the executive, and Article III the judiciary. It was designed as a checks and balances system to protect against a single branch or dictator taking control of the government. Considering world history up to that point, the concept was brilliant. In the Trump era it is being put to the test.

The powers and purposes of each branch were carefully debated and negotiated. Until recently, the three branches have followed their constitutional duties and have worked reasonably well to co-govern the nation. It appears that at least a part of the legislative branch in the Trump era has willingly surrendered its coequal status and subordinated itself to the executive branch, thereby violating the letter and the spirit of the Constitution as so carefully designed by our Founding Fathers ("Republicans' choice: Stand with Trump or risk his wrath," *Politico*).

The Constitution probably would not have been ratified without the promise of a Bill of Rights, the first ten amendments to the Constitution. Passage of the Bill of Rights closely followed the signing of the Constitution, providing now-famous freedoms that have become the bedrock of the American experience:

➢ Prohibiting Congress from enacting any law "abridging the freedom of *speech*, or of the *press*; or the right of the people peaceably to *assemble*, and to petition the government for a redress of grievances."
➢ Prohibiting Congress from enacting any law "respecting an establishment of *religion*, or prohibiting the free exercise thereof."

➤ Guaranteeing "the right of the people to *keep and bear arms* shall not be infringed."

➤ Protection from "the unreasonable *search or seizure* of their persons, houses, papers and effects."

➤ "Nor shall private property be *taken* for public use, without just compensation."

➤ The "right to a speedy and public *trial*, by an impartial jury."

➤ "To have the assistance of *counsel* for his defense."

➤ The prohibition against "*cruel and unusual punishment.*"

➤ Protection against "*double jeopardy.*"

➤ The right against "*self incrimination.*"

The freedoms contained in the Bill of Rights are a blessing and a right for which all Americans should be grateful. Initially, "all citizens" meant all white males. Women had to wait well over a century to be allowed to have a voice. African Americans and Native Americans were not considered people and were initially accorded no rights. It has been a long and rocky road for these groups to attain a place at the table for an opportunity to be free to pursue their American dreams of life, liberty, and happiness.

The leading advocates for civil rights, women's rights, LGTBQ rights, and Native American rights are taking their place alongside the Founding Fathers as powerful forces responsible for moving American history in the direction of a nation in alignment with its core values.

So the system is in place for a free and just nation. America has come a long way on this road to respecting the values we hold dear, and it still has a long way to go in reaching its goals. It is a process that has, and will, take centuries to fully evolve.

The road is filled with political potholes, twisting turns, and construction barricades. There is no designated "finish line."

America's Many Blessings

Most Americans freely acknowledge that the United States of America, though not perfect, is as good as it gets in an imperfect world. We enjoy endless freedoms, choices, and opportunities. Our standard of living provides many Americans with comfortable lives that include an education, work and careers, food, shelter, health care, entertainment, friendships, information, technology, travel and transportation, financial security, and a relatively safe and stable environment. America is a country that people want to get into, not to escape from. It is a place where people have the opportunity to grow, evolve, and enjoy life.

As we approach two and a half centuries of history, the current generation has an obligation to preserve and protect America's resources and freedoms for future generations. Our children and grandchildren also deserve to enjoy the "American experience." We cannot afford to ignore, deny, or overlook the treasure that we have been given. It is one of those things worth fighting for.

Trumpian Blessings

Based on his behavior, tweets, and facial expressions, Donald J. Trump does not appear to be a happy camper. His only blessings involve "winning" at someone else's expense. There is no awareness or appreciation for the wealth and privileged life he has been given—only resentments for failing to gain the respect of so many people.

Mental health professionals have offered explanations of Trump's state of mind. For whatever reason, he has chosen anger, threats, revenge, bullying, lying, cheating, and other forms of fear as his mode of operation. It is a mode that precludes an awareness of true blessings.

An Awareness

We see the world through our own unique eyesight. What we see is the result of the thoughts and the choices we make in our mind's eye. Our thoughts determine our reality.

We can choose to see the Trump era as an attack on basic universal values, or we can see this time as an opportunity to clearly see the difference between love and fear. This era can provide the contrast that is needed to begin the healing process. For this awareness we can choose to be thankful. We have the power to "make America grateful again."

Closing Thoughts

I did not experience military service in my youth. Writing this book as an adult is my way of fighting for the future of America. It is my way of expressing my patriotism. To be clear, I am not being critical of America or its people. I am being critical of Donald Trump's behavior and policies as president of my country. Since I am a white guy who was born in America, I trust that President Trump will not urge me to "go back to that "s---hole"" I came from ("Republicans are quiet as Trump urges four minority congresswomen to leave the country," *Washington Post July 15, 2019*).

We don't have to be an academic, government specialist, psychiatrist, psychologist, mental health counselor, journalist, or wannabe politician in order to express our opinions. I know many concerned Americans who are keenly aware of the current state and possible future direction of America in the Trump era. Like them, I was disappointed and worried following the surprise election of President Trump on that November day in 2016.

A believer in fair play, it never dawned on me that a hostile foreign government might have influenced the election results or that an American presidential campaign would be open and welcoming to such foreign interference.

Since the inauguration, my concerns have deepened considerably. As the Mueller report confirms, the level of conduct in the Oval Office has approached criminal status, and the bar of acceptable presidential behavior has been set at an incredibly low level.

This book represents my thoughts, feelings, and fears about where our country appears to be going on this journey with Trump at the helm. Ultimately you, the reader, are your own judge and jury. How America is moving forward (or backward) is a matter of personal perspective.

American values are really in the eyes of the beholders. One person may view an athlete kneeling during the National Anthem as an act of treason; another may view it as upholding the precious American right of freedom of expression. One person may see a migrant caravan moving through Central America toward the US border as a terrorist threat; another may see women and children desperately fleeing violence and gang warfare in their native country, seeking safety and asylum in the United States of America. One person may see lying, cheating, obstructing, and misleading as effective leadership tools; another may see such threatening conduct as criminal, or at the very least, below acceptable standards of the office of president.

The ball is now in our court to determine where America goes from here. May God bless America!

Jim Boeglin, JD